Best Wishes
Mike Field

The Museum of Figments
© 2021 Mister Finch

Photography and story by Mister Finch
Layout and design by Graham Pilling / Army of Cats Creative Studio

All rights reserved. No part of this book may be reproduced, stored in a retrieval system, or transmitted in any form or by any means, mechanical, photocopying, recording or otherwise, without the prior permission of the copyright owner.

ISBN 978-1-3999-0116-1

First printing in the United Kingdom 2021.

www.mister-finch.com

Welcome to The Museum of Figments

1. What are Figments? 8
2. Felicitys 11
3. Potion of the Circle 26
4. Housies 31
5. Red Rings 44
6. Chanters 47
7. Gillypillys 59
8. The Brass Book 70
9. Gardenias 73
10. Twice 90
11. Cupboardies 95
12. Candle Snuffer Wands 112
13. Stories 117
14. Children's Rhyme 138

What are Figments?

Well, to answer this question, we must first introduce you to a certain type of witch.

A Thimble Witch — or 'Thimbles' as they are affectionately known to their friends.

A Thimble Witch is a curious creature. All witches have their own, unique talents, yes, but Thimbles are known for doing things a little differently. Incredibly creative, these witches like to constantly busy themselves, making things.

True to their name, they do indeed use a thimble when creating, and of course, they often use a needle and thread. But their creativity doesn't stop at simply sewing. Oh no. The Thimble Witch is crafty in every sense of the word.

Busy, busy, always so busy.

Maybe you know one?

As we all know, it is usual for a witch to have a familiar — a cat, a toad or maybe an owl. And this is where we start to really see why Thimbles are so very different.

Thimble Witches make their own helpers.

They create their own Familiar.

These creations are called Figments.

Figments are only born by the hands of a Thimble Witch and only Thimbles truly know the magic required to make them.

Curiosities and oddments, seemingly commonplace to the untrained eye, are carefully chosen to create these little helpers. Thimble Witches have often been known to use sentimental objects, clothing or even heirloom jewellery to make these helpers incredibly personal for the recipient. Lovingly stitched or carved, whittled and sometimes even baked, making a Figment in a certain style or manner will ensure the kind of helper needed is created.

A witch needing a little more help than others, or one who has found themselves sadly alone, has the ability to fabricate Twin Figments. This is seen as a truly wonderful omen. Fondly called *Twigments*, these helpers often mirror each other's movements and hand gestures in a delightful and almost kaleidoscopic way.

Once they are made, a Figment is brought to life with a spell and a magical liquid called *'Potion of the Circle'*.*

Some Figments are made by family or friends, some are given as gifts. Some are bought ready-made from spell shops and others are ordered in the post from far away countries. There is an amazing community of Thimble Witches, who do nothing other than create Figments for others. This is why they vary so much and ultimately arrive to those in need through lots of different avenues.

---

* See *'Potion of the Circle,'* page 26

Figments run around our world. In and out of shadows they go, dashing around doing all manner of jobs and activities. Moving at lightning speed, most non-magical folk just never see them.

They may glimpse something from the corner of their eye...

Or was it just a trick of the light?

Maybe it was a bird or an insect?

Maybe it's because my eyes are tired...?

I'm sure I saw something... I did... it was fast... something... just there for a split second... maybe it was a mere figment of my imagination?

Or maybe, it was indeed, a Figment.

About the Museum

The museum itself has been in operation since the early 1900s.

Often moving around in secret, at one time it was said to have found its place behind an old staircase, in a rental property in London.

Set up by a small group of Thimble Witches, the museum was initially used as a place to store and collect magical artifacts and books, but it very quickly became the resting place Figments sought when their owner had sadly died.

You see, the potion used to bring the Figment to life doesn't last forever; there's only a small amount of time until the Potion of the Circle wears off.

Think of it like a clockwork toy that has wound down but instead of springs and cogs, here there is magic.

Here at the museum our cabinets and shelves are filled to the brim with these fantastical beings. They gaze out from behind glass, in their unwound clockwork sleepy silence.

Many Figments find their own way to the museum, and some are donated. They often arrive carrying personal possessions from their owners' homes. However, some don't quite make it, their magic runs out too quickly and they sadly end up lost in the world, or find themselves labelled as a strange doll in an antique shop.

It is easy to see why people may view the museum as a sad place, full of treasures left behind. It can be hard to come to terms with the stillness of Figments.

Whilst this is true, here at the museum, we like to look at it quite differently.

We see it as a celebration of a magical life. And the museum, our museum, is a special place to hold, display and respect treasured Figments.

A place where magic is always still bubbling, just beneath the surface.

Often confused with creatures from the fairy realm, Felicitys are slim and elegant with very fast-moving wings.

Highly sociable, they are favoured by a witch who prefers the old ways and more traditional magic. They make light work of stitching and when in groups, they can complete large needlework projects at alarming rates.

Often very mischievous by nature but great all-rounders.

Bed belonging to a Felicity.
Donated to the Museum in 1985.

Potion of the Circle

This potion has an incredibly magical ingredient. It is at the very heart of our story and is the reason these magical helpers can be brought to life.
Without it we would have no Figments and no museum.

The folklore of the potion's creation has many versions, but most tales are told something like this...

It's late autumn and a small group of fishermen's wives sing while they mend nets, work rope into complex knots and sweep the sand from their thick aprons.

An amber sun sets slowly in a pink sky, gulls cry out overhead... all is still.

The gathered women have wise eyes which truly understand the beauty of the ocean.

Honest eyes, which confess the pain of waiting and worrying for loved ones. It's what brings these women close, it holds them firm, and keeps them strong, together, when times are hard.

The smell of sea salt mixes with the small crackling fire.

Suddenly their laughter and singing is broken by a loud splashing far in the distance...

The eldest of the women quickly stands. With one hand to her brow, the other clutches her leather cape tightly.

She gasps as a large fishtail whips up from the waves.

'Quickly!' she says, pointing to a small rowboat.

The women climb aboard and with what seems like effortless haste, they reach the scene.

Something is trapped in a net, thrashing wildly.

The eldest takes out her knife and begins cutting the grid of rope. She is fast and calm in this chaotic scene.

But this is no fish. It is a mermaid, and her face, just below the water's surface, is pleading for help.

The other women scramble to help free the creature, desperately pulling and tugging on the ropes and nets until eventually she is released.

They collapse, soaked, in the boat and for a moment all is eerily still. The women look at each other, panting and confused.

They break the silence with tentative laughter from sheer relief and gaze back over the side of the boat.

The now free mermaid is swimming in circles below, slowly moving up towards the surface which is littered with rope fragments and large clear fish scales.

Finally, her head bobbing up, she reveals her ghostly pale face, set with large emerald-green eyes.

She smiles and nods to the women.

'Thank you, my sisters', she says, relieved.

The women reach towards her and, one by one, touch her hand.

It is a moment of mutual understanding and gratitude.

'Is there anything I can do to repay you?' the mermaid asks, wiping her kelp-green hair from her face.

'Not unless you know of a quick way for us to repair our nets...?' the eldest woman jokes.

The mermaid looks to the sky as if in thought and simply says, 'Maybe I can help...'

She turns quickly and dives into the inky depths, her tail showing a brief glimpse of dark yellow spots and spirals of barnacles.

A few minutes pass and the mermaid reappears at the side of the boat. She reaches out her webbed hand and passes a fistful of red stones to one of the women.

'Sea garnets', she says. 'Take them.'

'Thank you. They are beautiful,' the woman replies, handing a stone to each of the others.

'Yes indeed', says the mermaid, 'but also very powerful. You can use them in your *spells*.'

The mermaid, recognising these magical women as witches, gazes at them as they each turn the stones between their fingers, the red-wine facets of the gems catching the setting sun.

'You need help with your nets... you can get help... you can "*make*" help. These stones, along with the right incantations, can make a potion that will bring things to life,' the mermaid explains.

'It can make a soup ladle sing or make your father's handkerchief dance a merry jig. You women are deft with a knife... Whittle some limbs, a body, and a head from wood; use scraps to make clothes. Make a small being, a child, a helper or a creature and then bring it to life,' she says excitedly.

'You can have helpers, all of you...' she adds. 'Tiny carved fingers can help you make your nets, darn the socks or help you stir the cooking pot.'

So that's how it all began. Or so the story goes...

These hard-working witches, their fingers always in tatters, became known as Thimble Witches due to their skills with winding ropework and intricately woven nets.

Thimble Witches, who were given the special gift of Figment conjuring, through one small, swift act of kindness...

The relationship between Mermaid and witch has continued for many, many years.

Those witches who can't get to the sea, know of places where garnets are sprinkled on foreshores and riverbeds by their sea-maiden friends. These red treasures can always be picked up and collected... if you know where to look.

The Largest Sea garnets are saved as talismans and often set into jewellery.*

The Potion of the Circle can be bought from all good spell shops, but homemade recipes are favoured and prove to be incredibly potent!

* See '*Red Rings*,' page 44

27

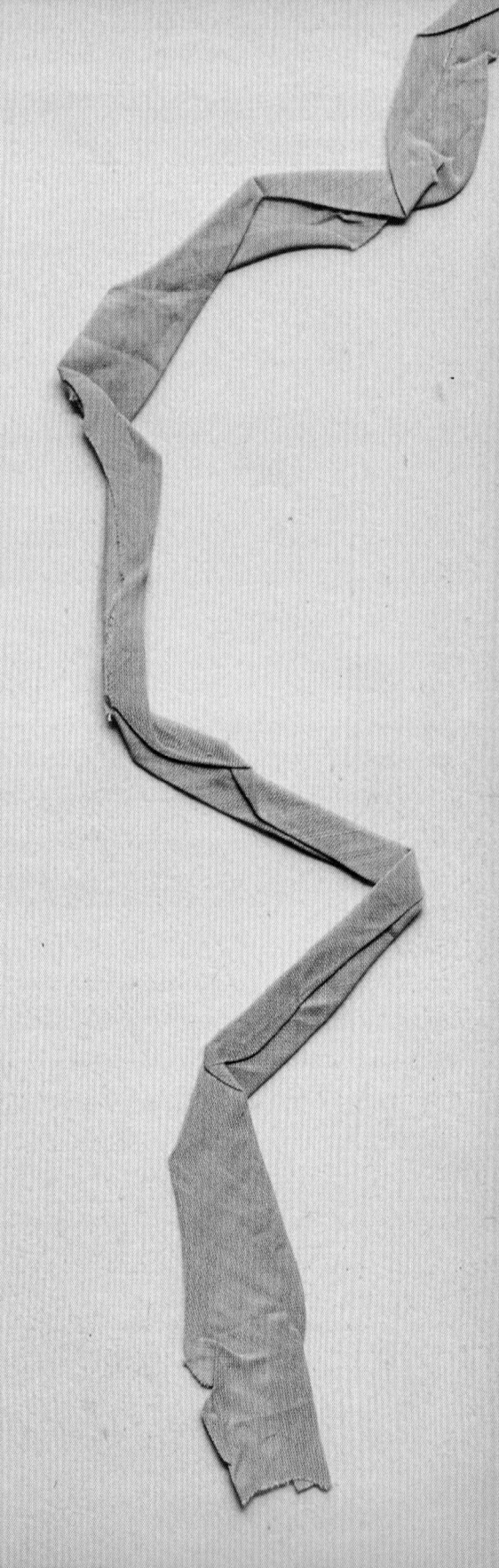

T hese figments, as the name suggests, are helpers and companions around the home. Wonderfully talented in the kitchen, their cooking and baking skills are second to none.
 Easily identifiable with their teapot or cup and saucer heads, Housies are warm and friendly and a delight to have around.

35

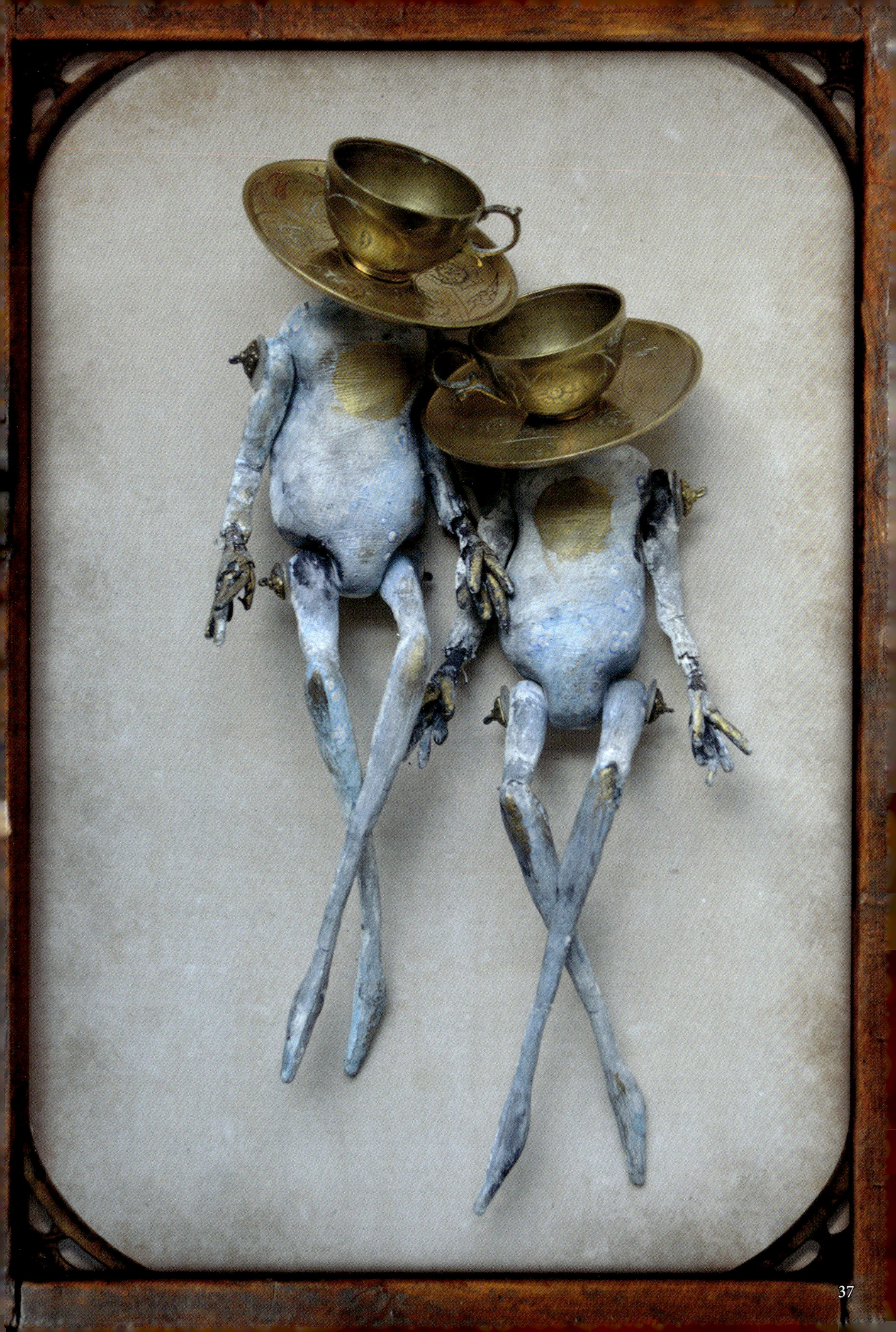

38

39

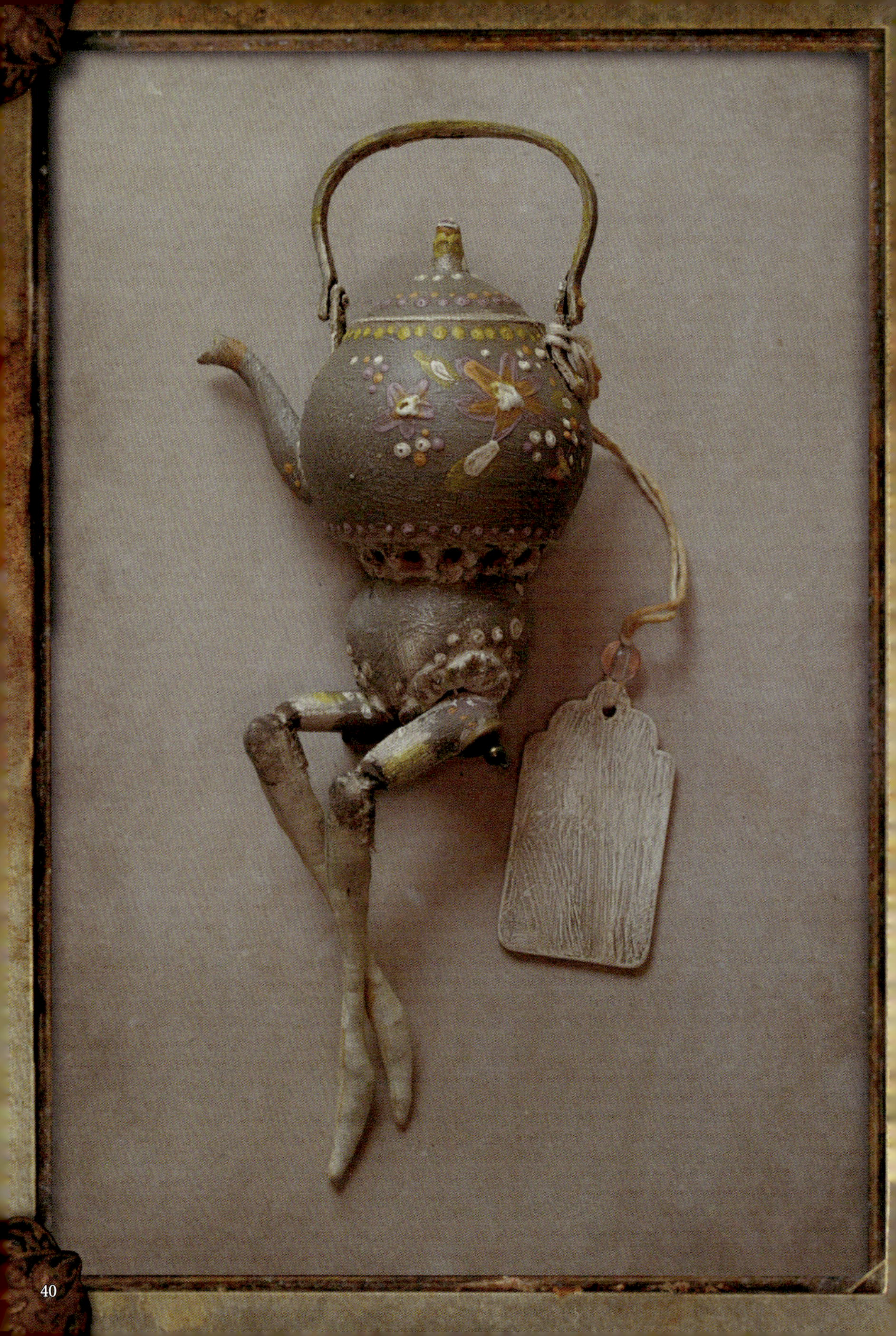

41

42

Collection of bottles used by Figments

Red Rings

The custom of Thimble Witches wearing a ring with a red stone is believed to go hand in hand with the story of our wonderful fisher women.*

Larger garnets were saved and set into rings, even then, as a symbol of their beliefs but more so as a way of recognising each other. When worn, these scarlet stones were said to bring the wearer peace and protection against illness, a belief that is still carried today.

Though modern-day versions rarely use real garnets anymore, the red stone remains a clear sign to others who dance within the magical circle.

The unique symbol of the red ring can be found painted or carved on old buildings and sometimes old trees, acting as pointers to meeting places and locations where spell ingredients are abundant.

It's very common for a Figment to arrive at the museum with their owner's ring.

* See 'Potion of the Circle,' page 26

45

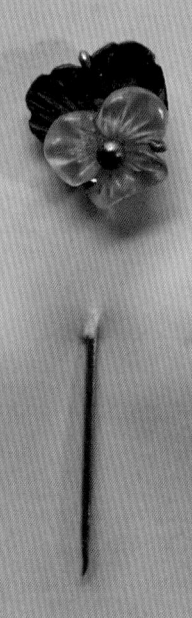

Chanters

Many witches are happy creating their own magic, others may need more help in conjuring. Chanters are a great fit for a young or beginner witch. Known for their incomparable knowledge of the magical arts and botanics, they are equally at home helping with studies as they are being outside foraging.

With wonderful insights in tarot and divination, these highly social Figments are fascinating company when in groups.

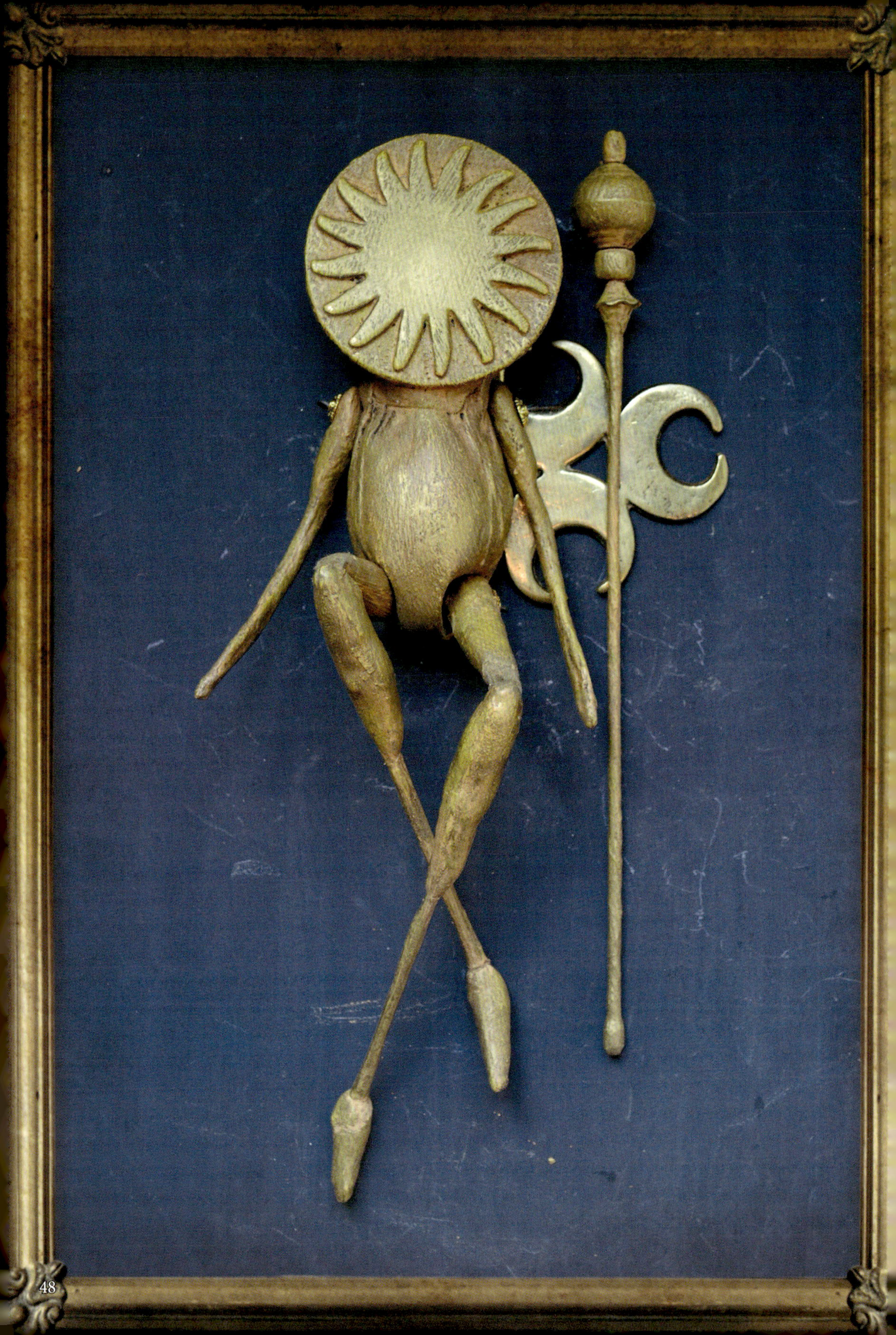

49

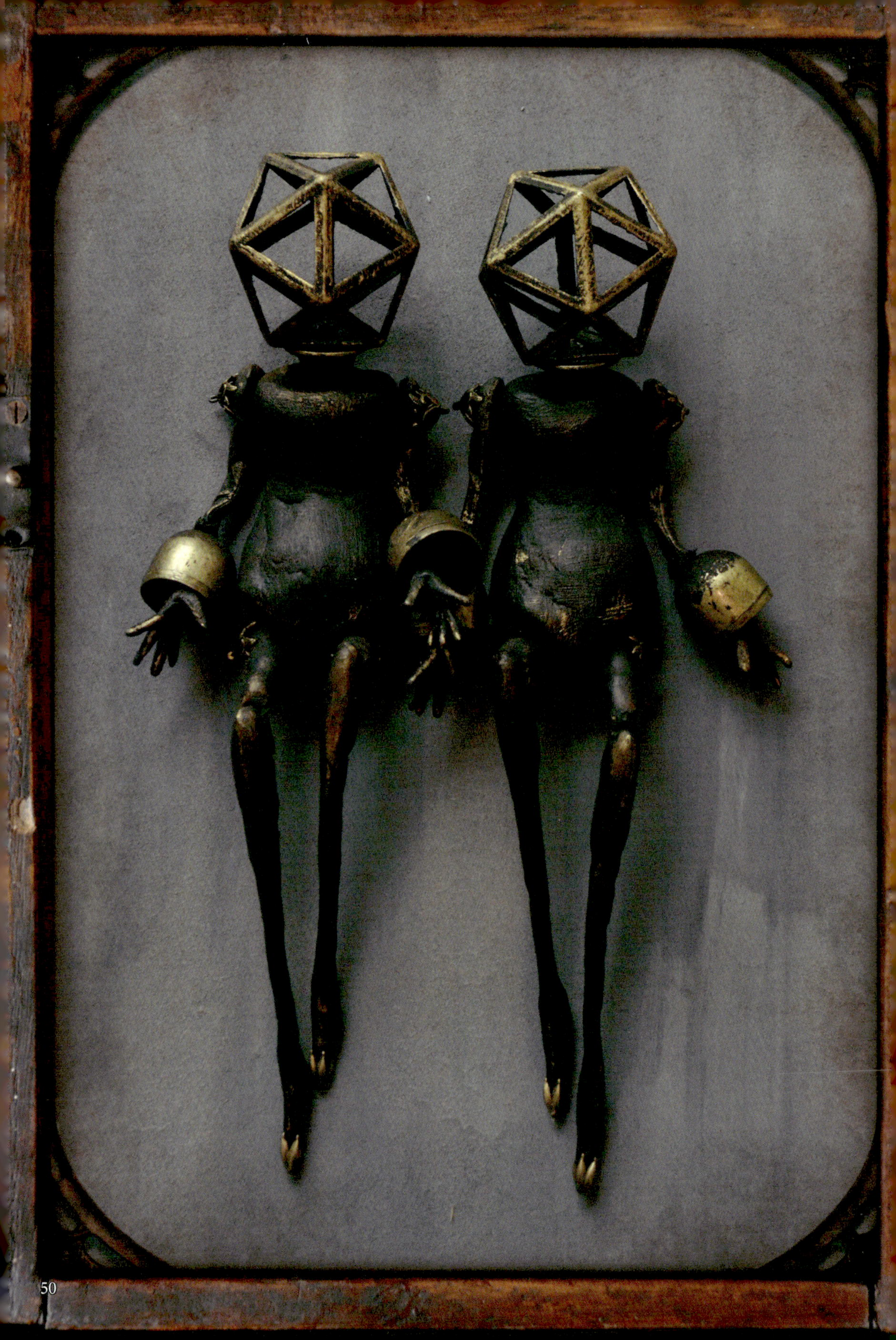

51

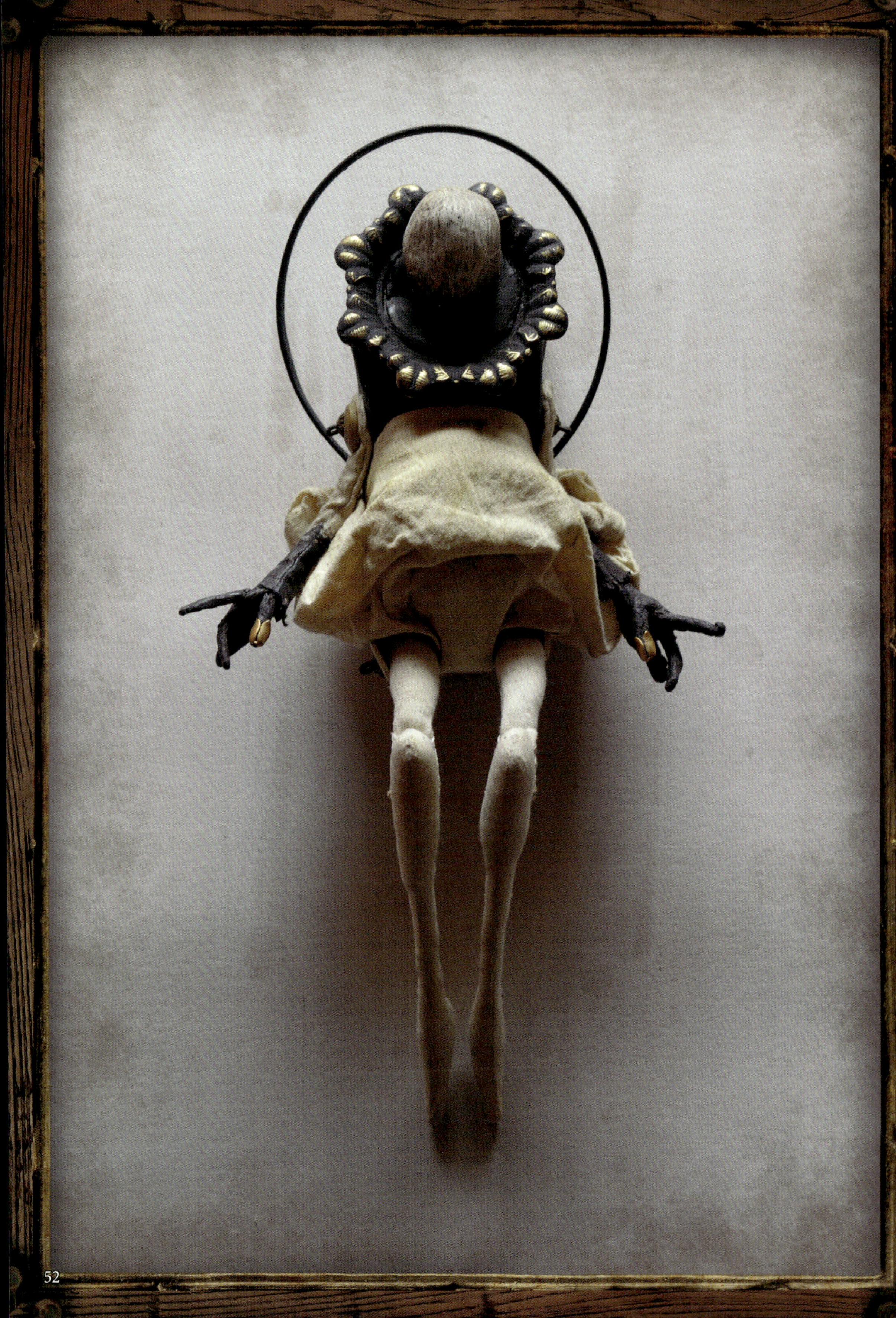

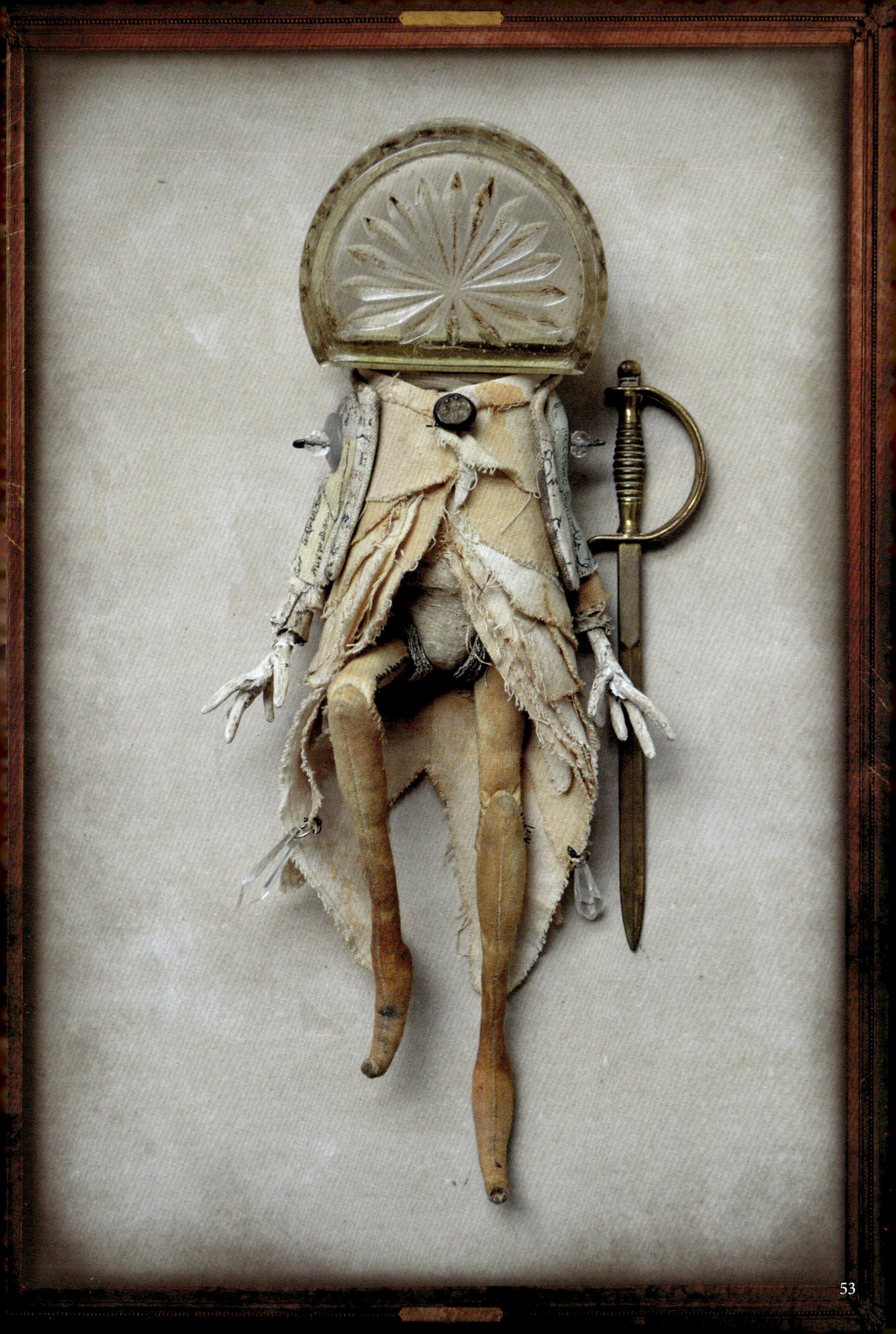

54

55

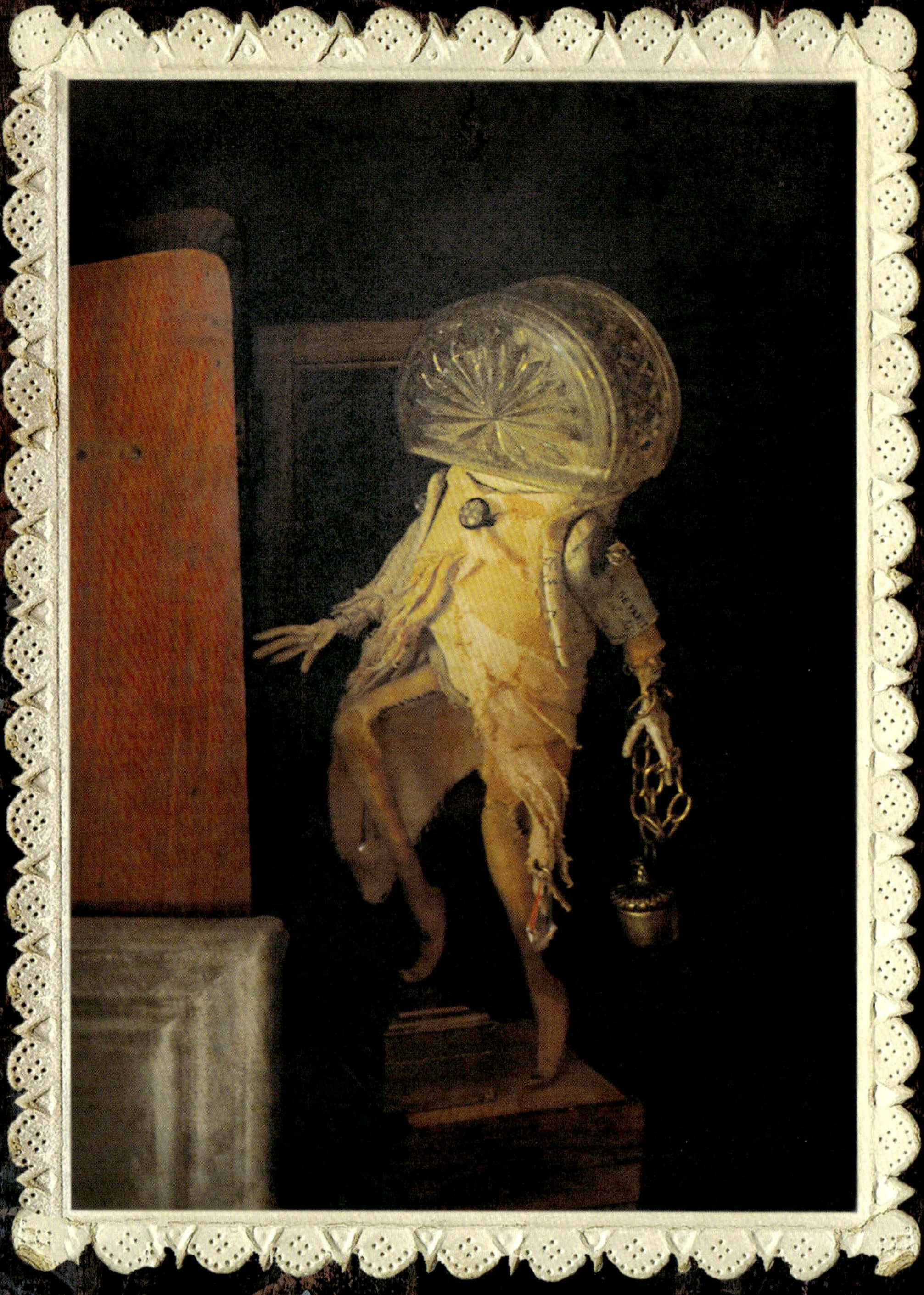

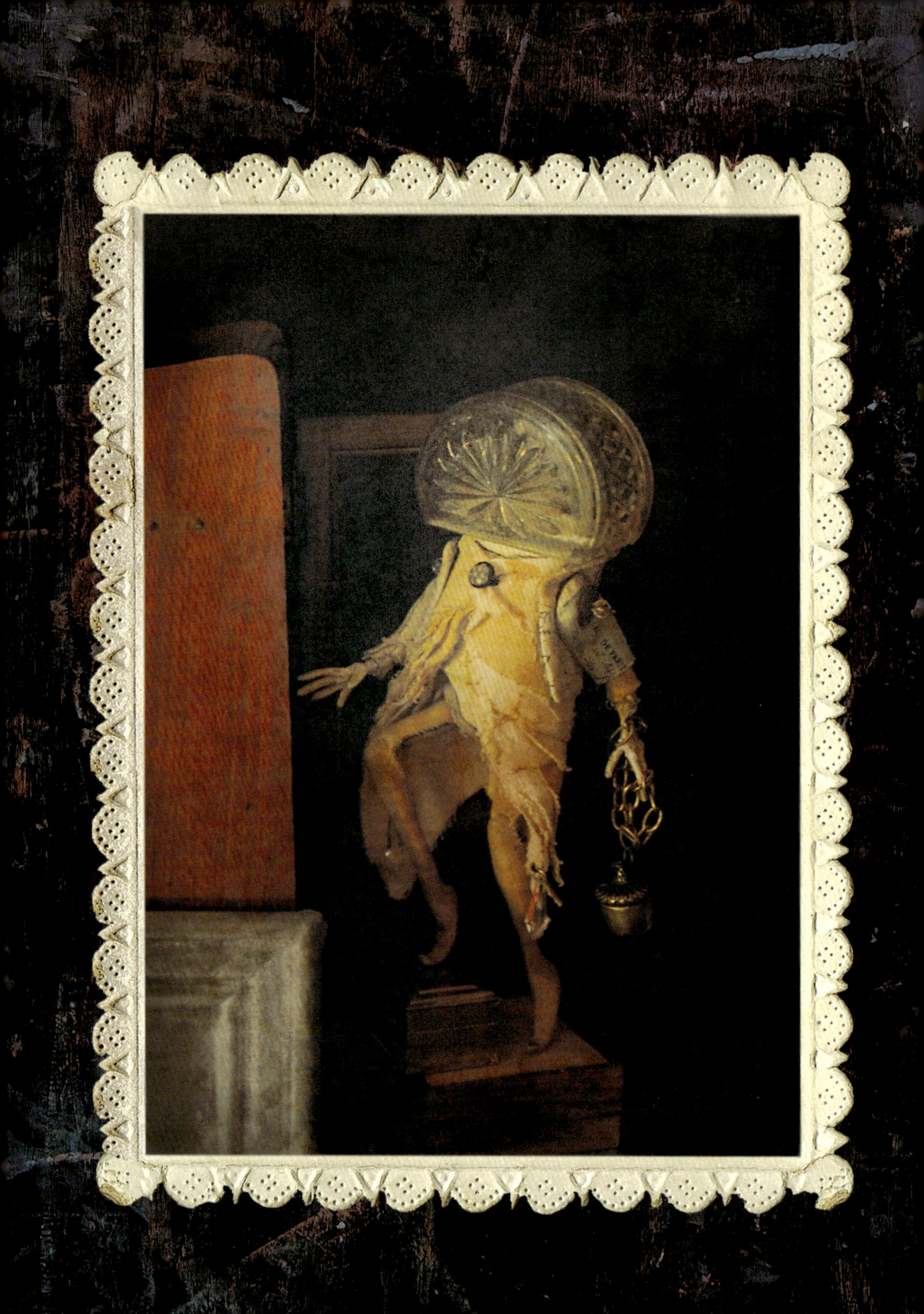

Chanter chair, very worn.

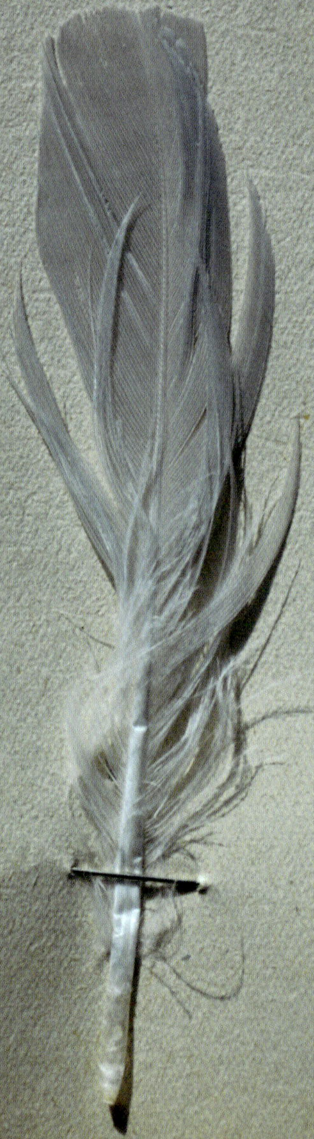

Gillypillys

Gillypillys are best suited to taking care of children and the elderly. They enjoy organising activities and are perfect for a very busy household with lots of children and pets.
Often taking the form of a recognisable animal or creature, you'd think they were easy to spot, but you'd be surprised…

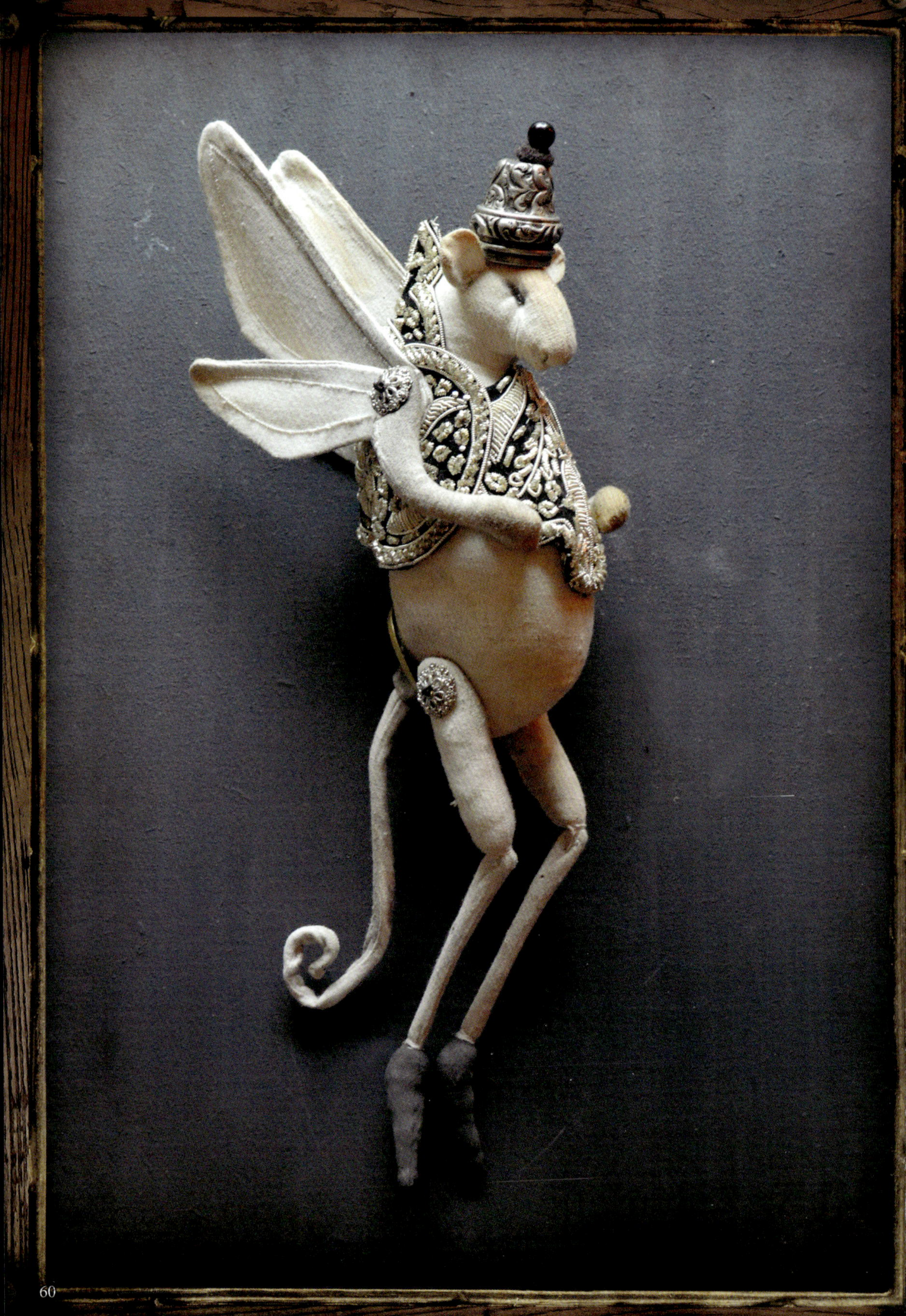

61

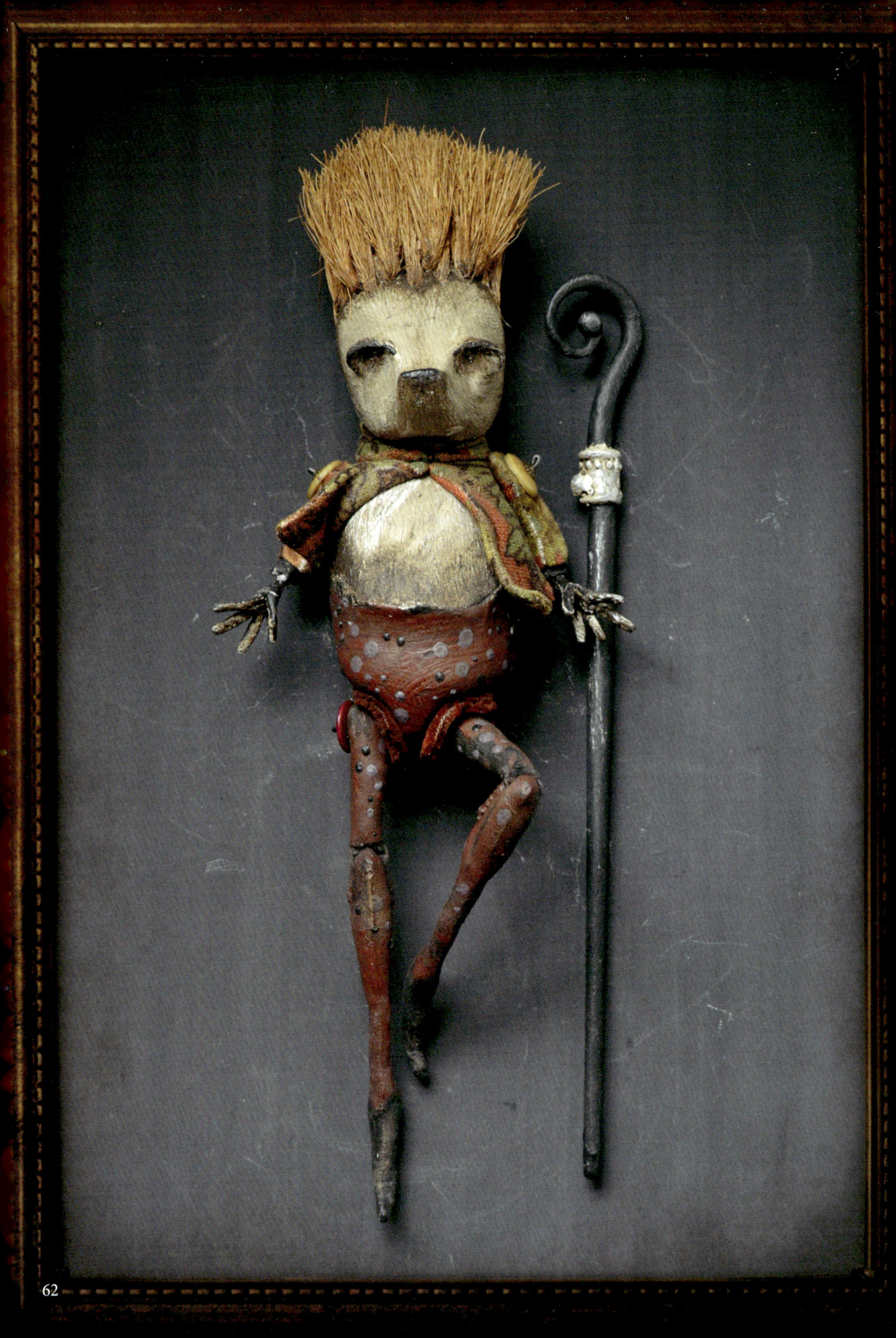

63

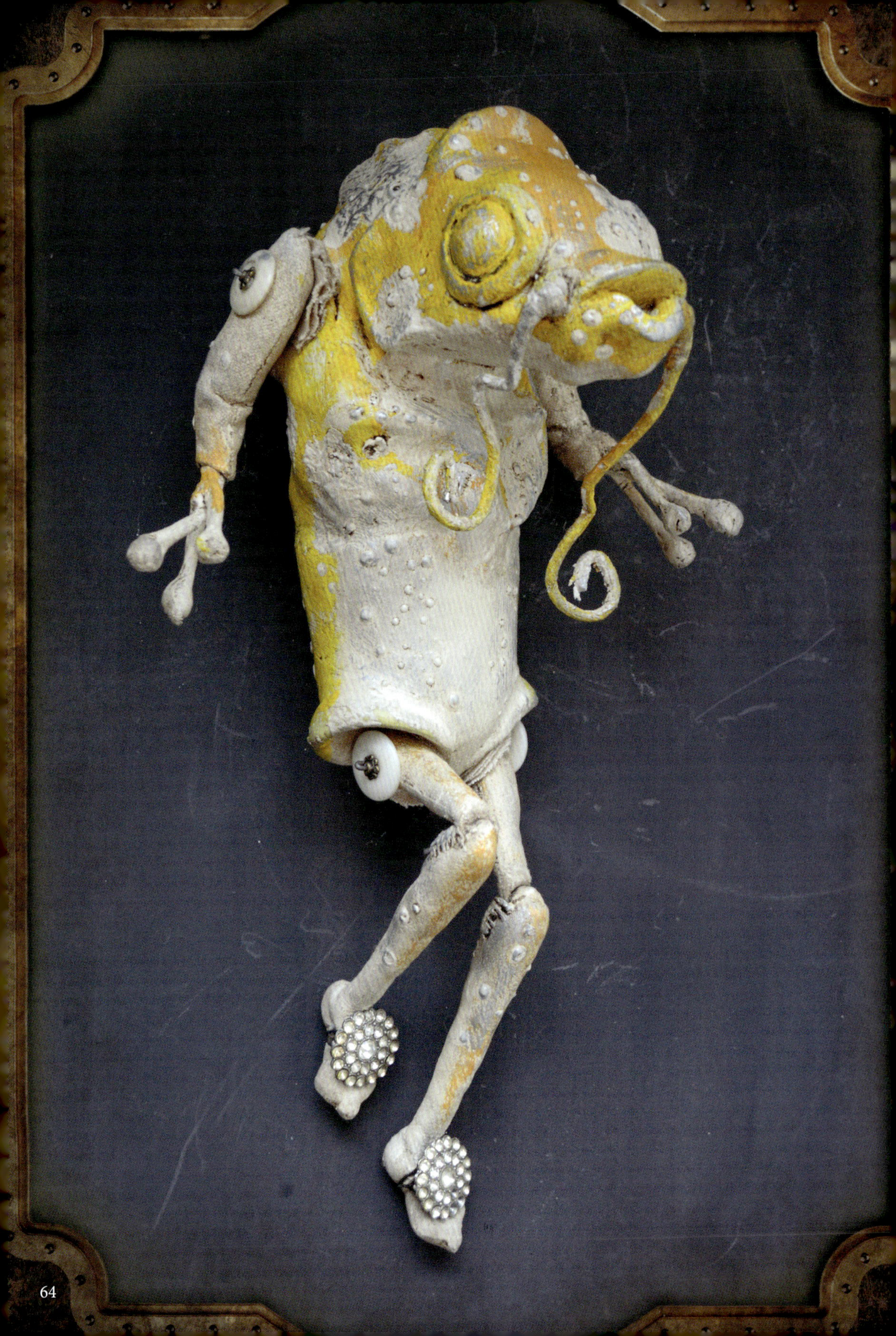

65

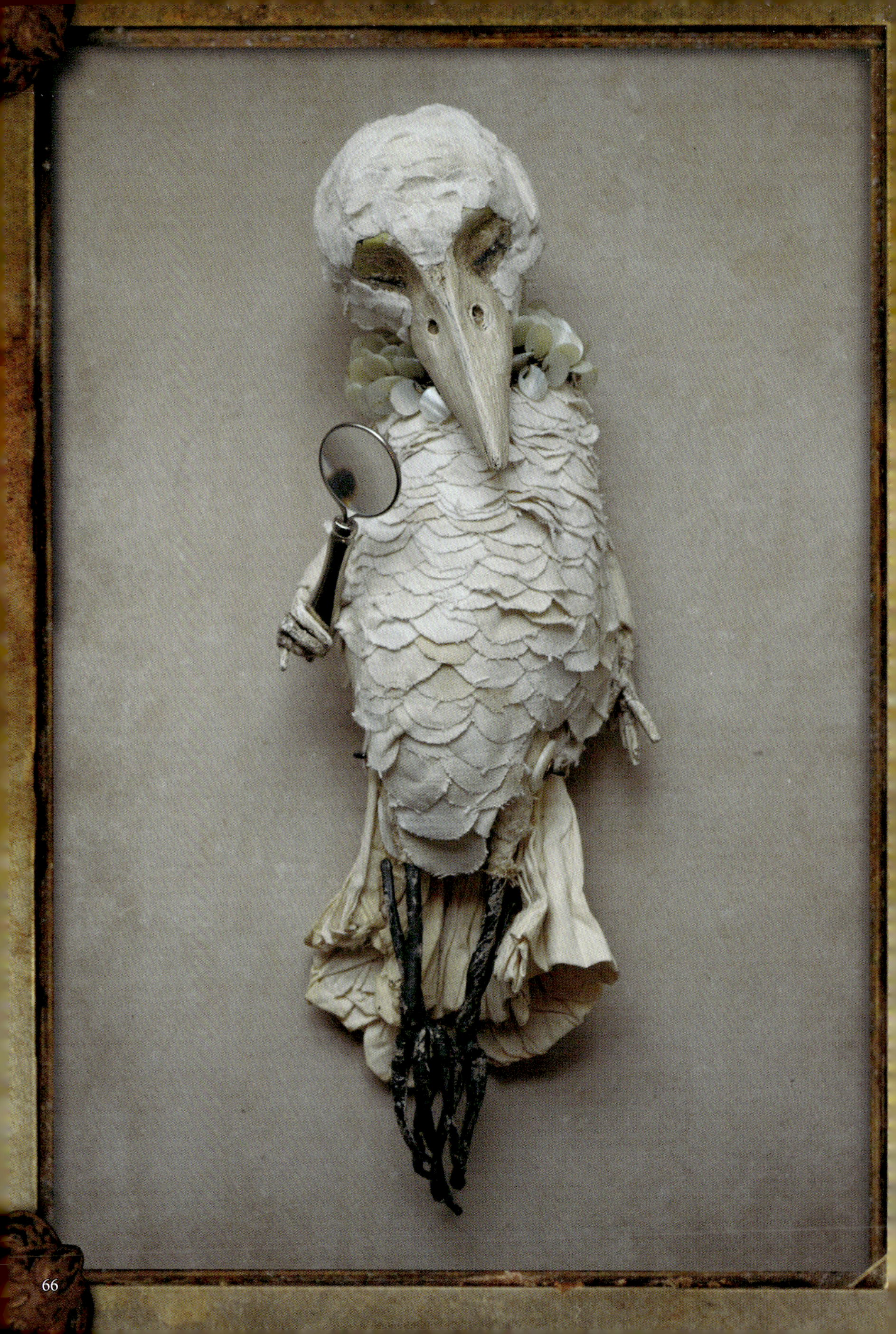

67

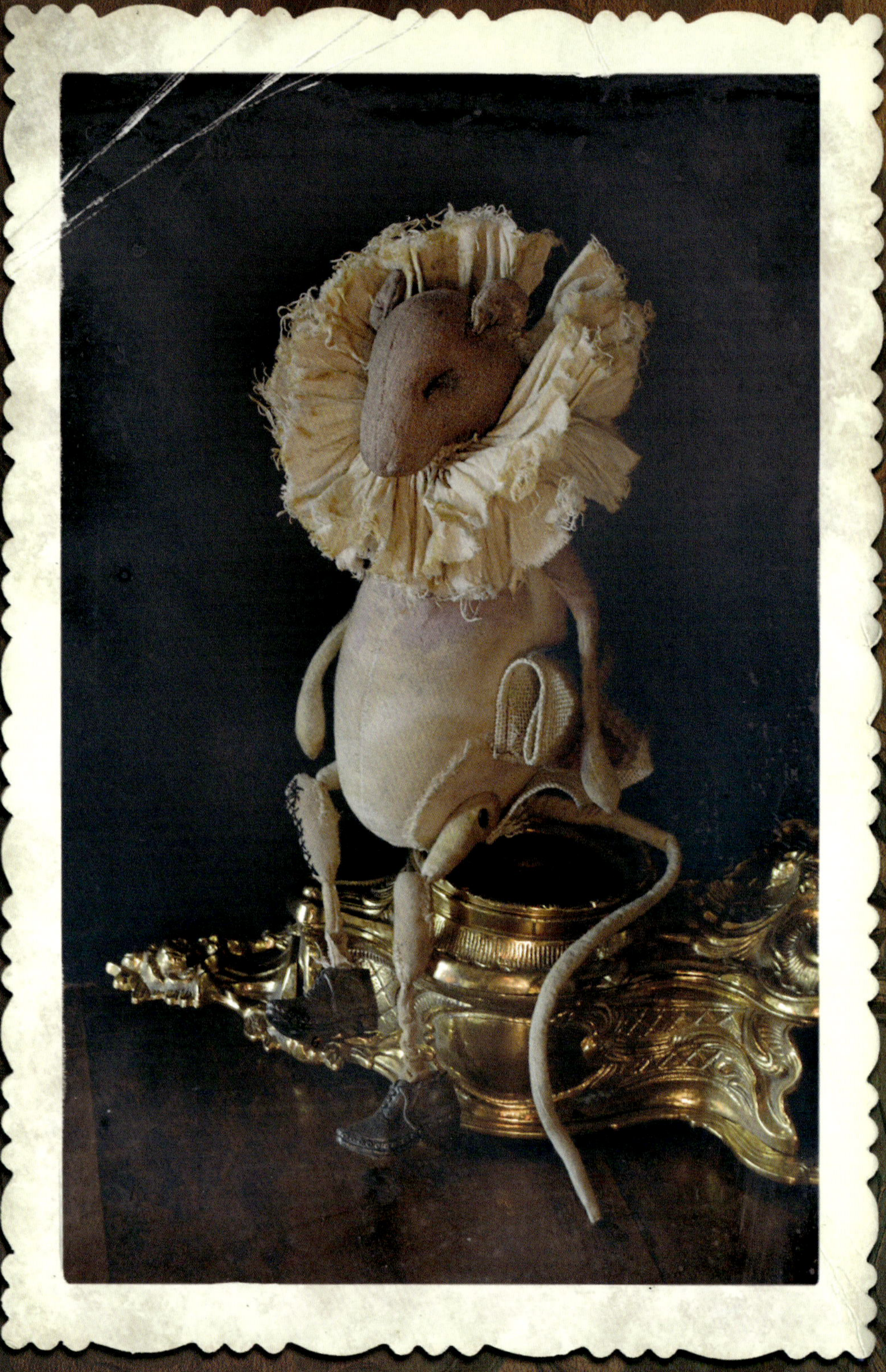

GILLYPILLY TEAPOT

The Brass Book

A Brass Book is one of the most precious and incredibly private possessions of a Thimble Witch. It holds their favourite spells and magical notes.

Chosen papers, diagrams and charts are neatly folded and held within, often with pressed flowers and leaves so that many become perfumed over the years.

Whilst not quite a book in the traditional sense, a Thimble Witch's Brass Book is a metal box made from brass or copper, featuring intricate flourishes and swirling scrolls.

They are kept about the person, sometimes worn around the neck on a chain. The act of polishing one on a lapel is a signal to other witches, and a secret language in itself.

A great many have been donated to the museum by family and friends. We treasure them here, and it seems a fitting place for secrets to remain secret, locked away.

Some families, however, traditionally hand down their Brass Books, especially those set with gemstones and sentimental engravings. In this event, any enclosed papers are buried with the deceased before the book is passed on to the next witch.

At many ceremonial locations and meeting places, witches are now requested to show a Red Ring[*] along with a Brass Book, in order to gain entrance. It is therefore customary, and almost imperative, for a Thimble Witch to never leave their home without both.

[*] See 'Red Rings,' page 44

71

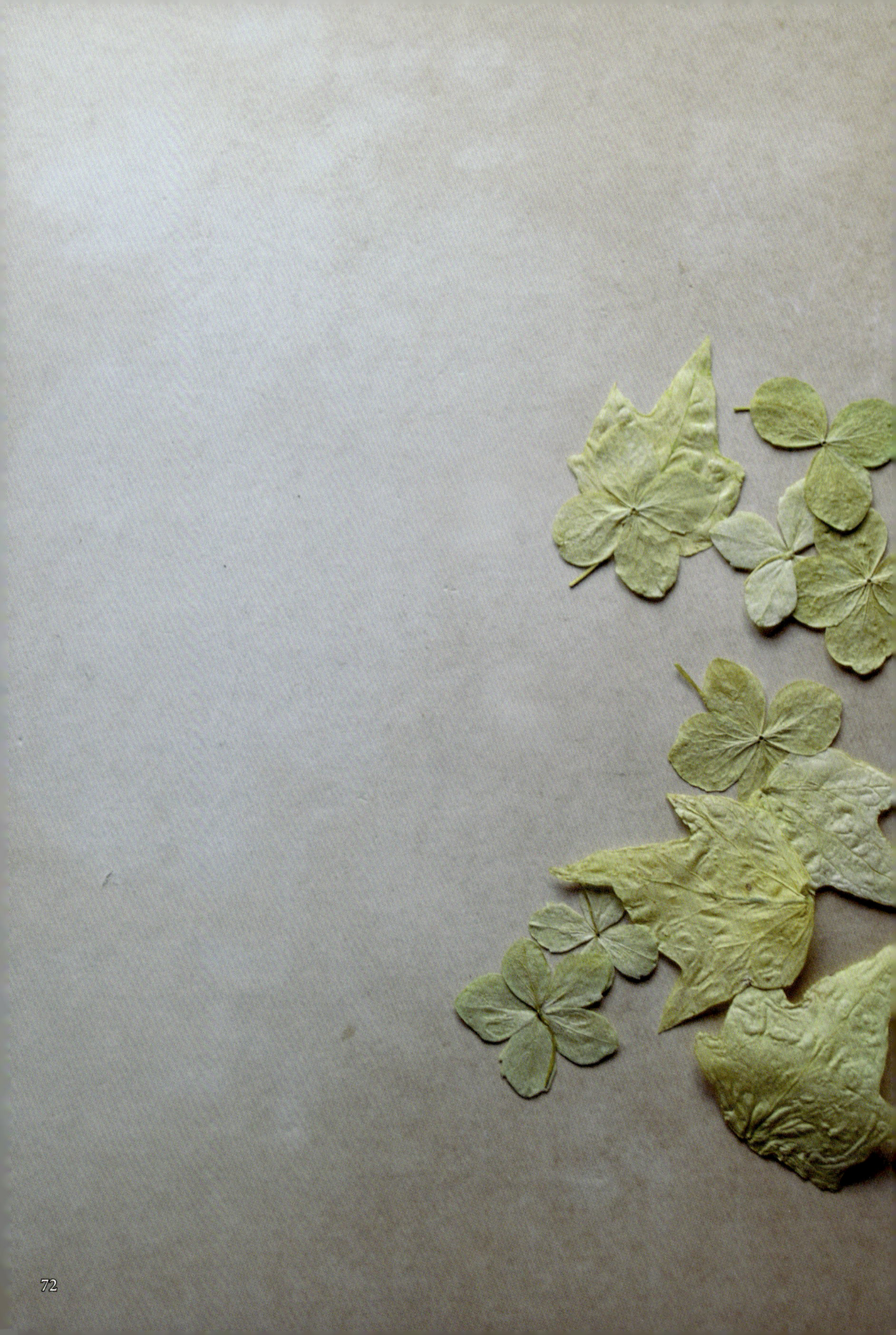

Gardenias

This unusual species can take the form of an insect or plant and sometimes a strange hybrid of both. They are most comfortable living outside, tending to flowers and vegetables.

Gardenias are a gentle workhorse, happiest when left to their own devices, and often heard singing whilst working.

Thriving best in homes with cats.

74

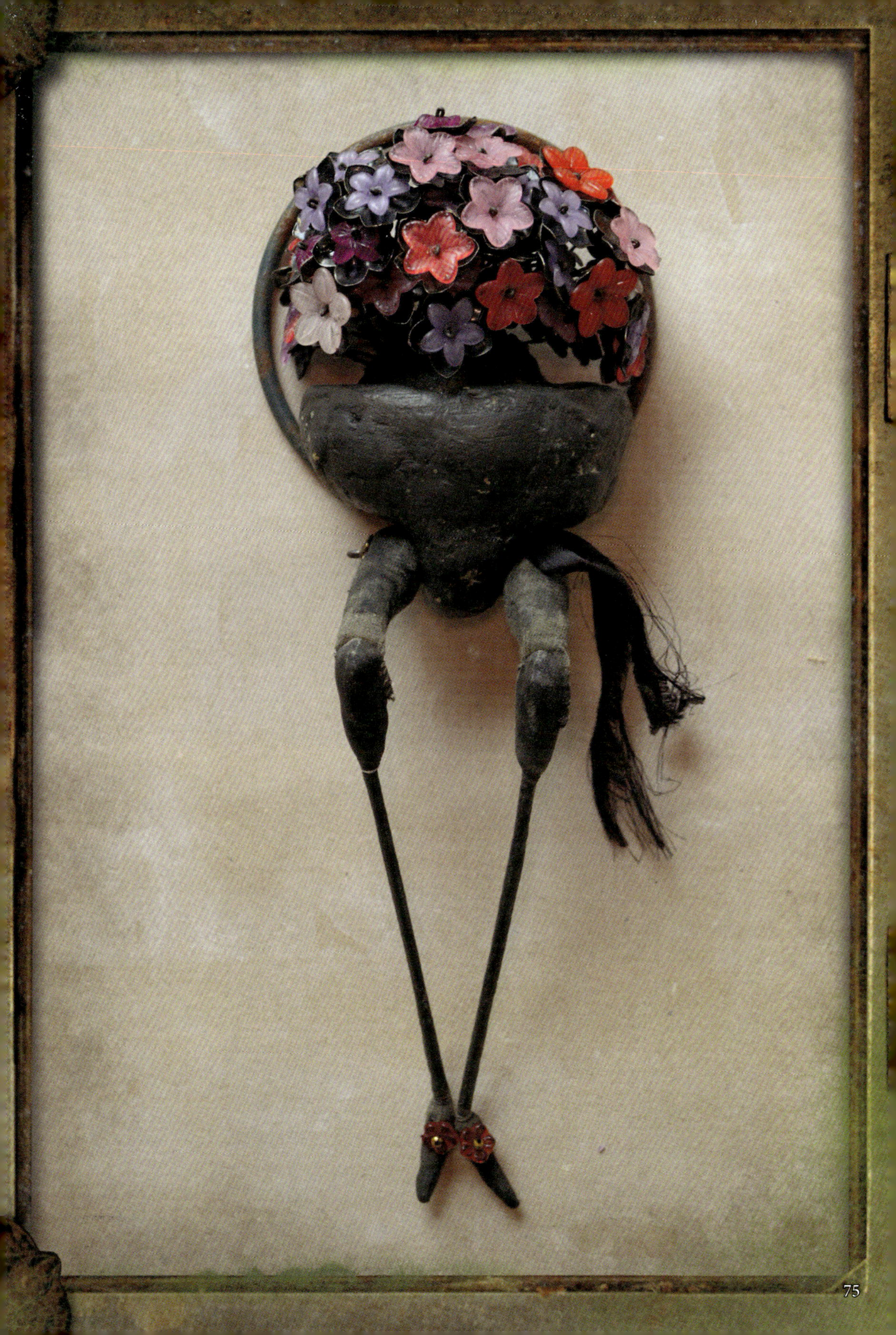

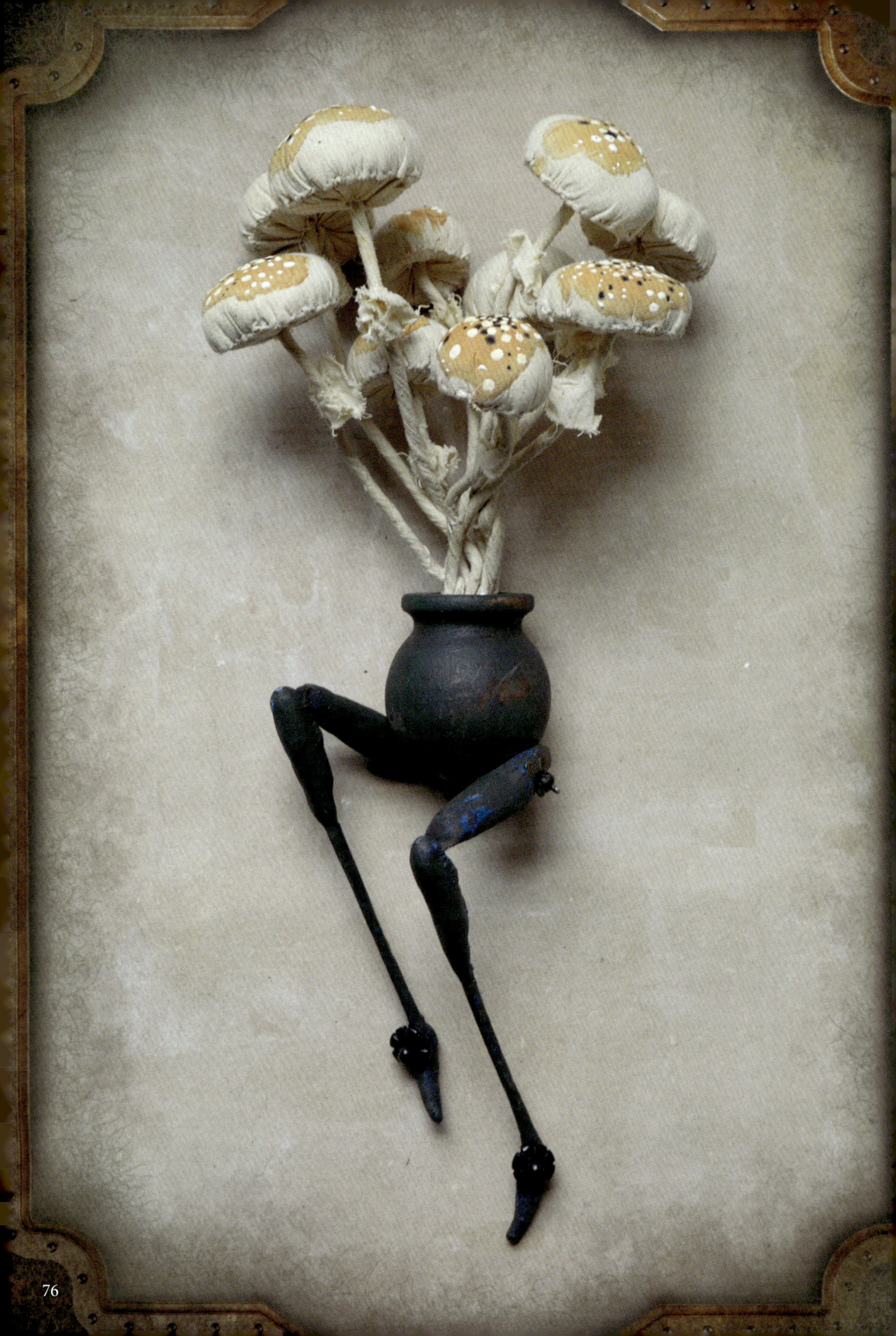

77

78

79

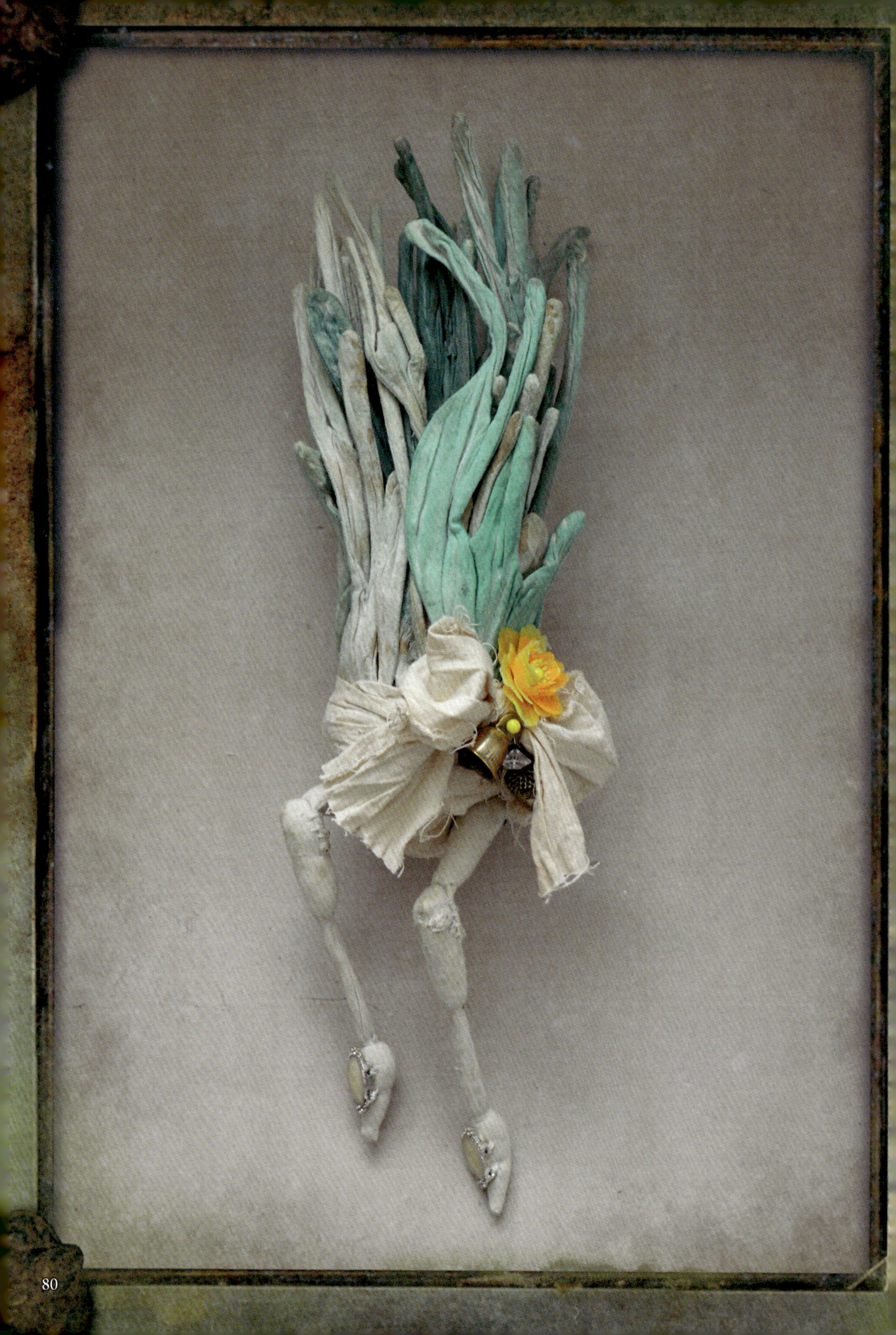

81

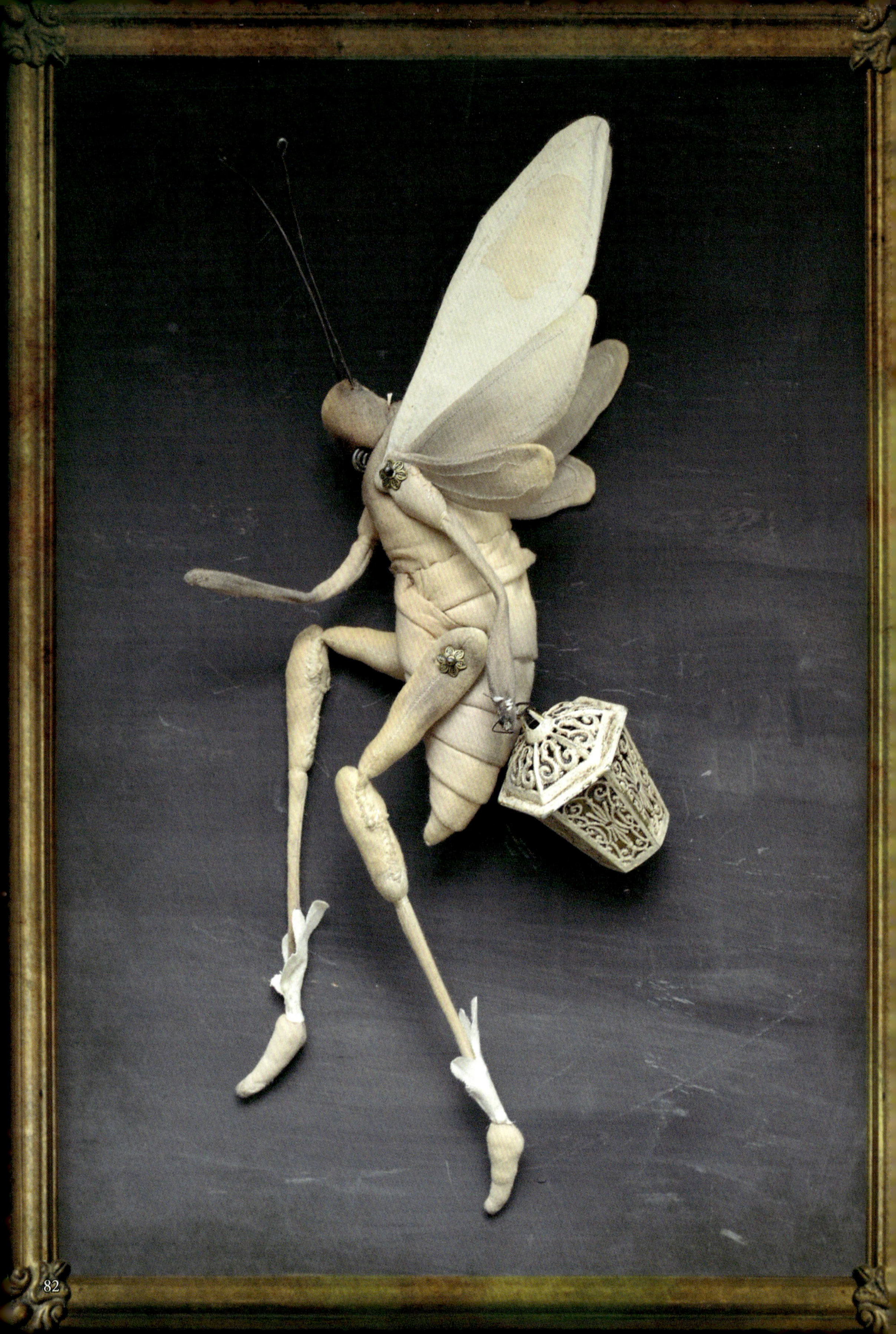

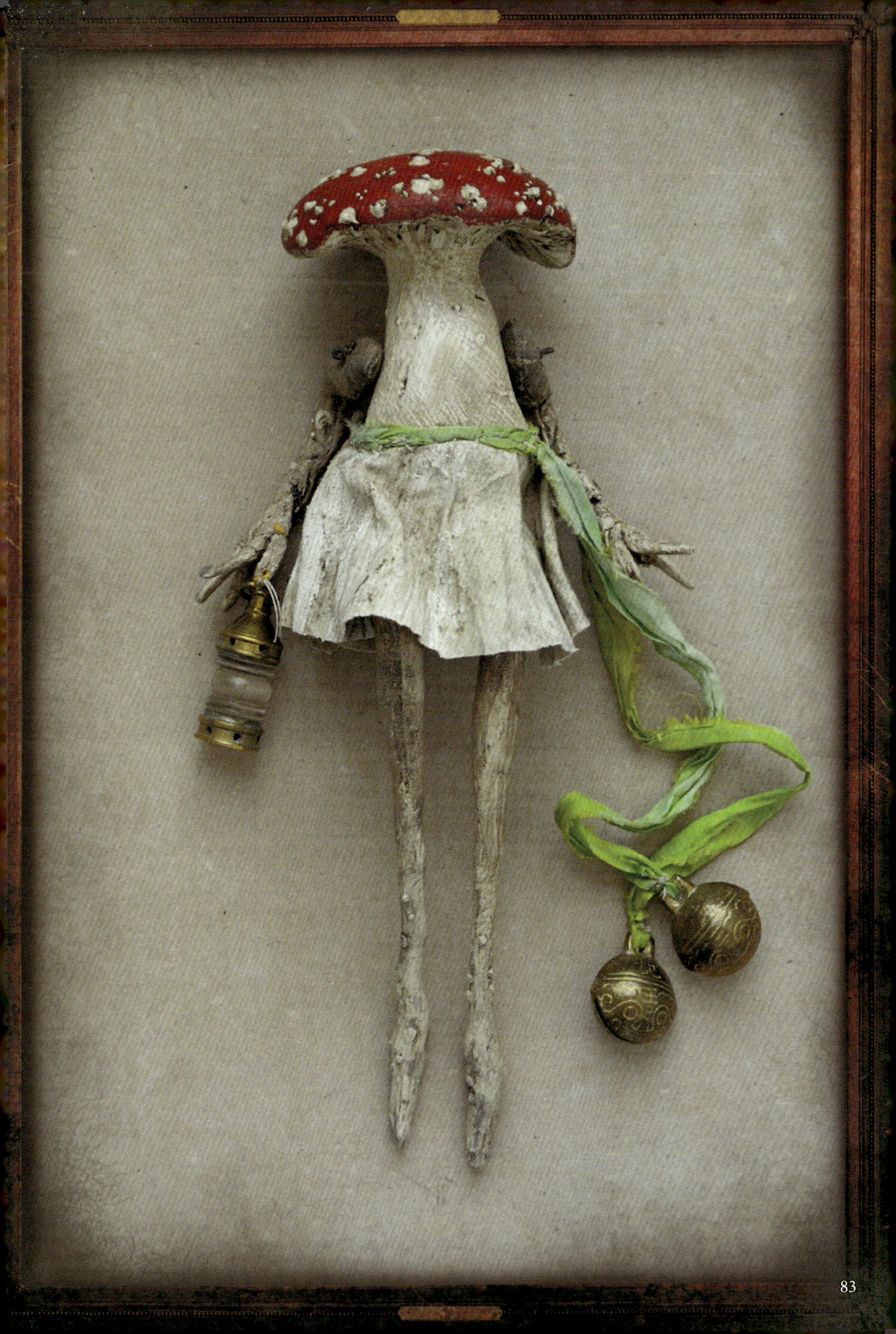

84

85

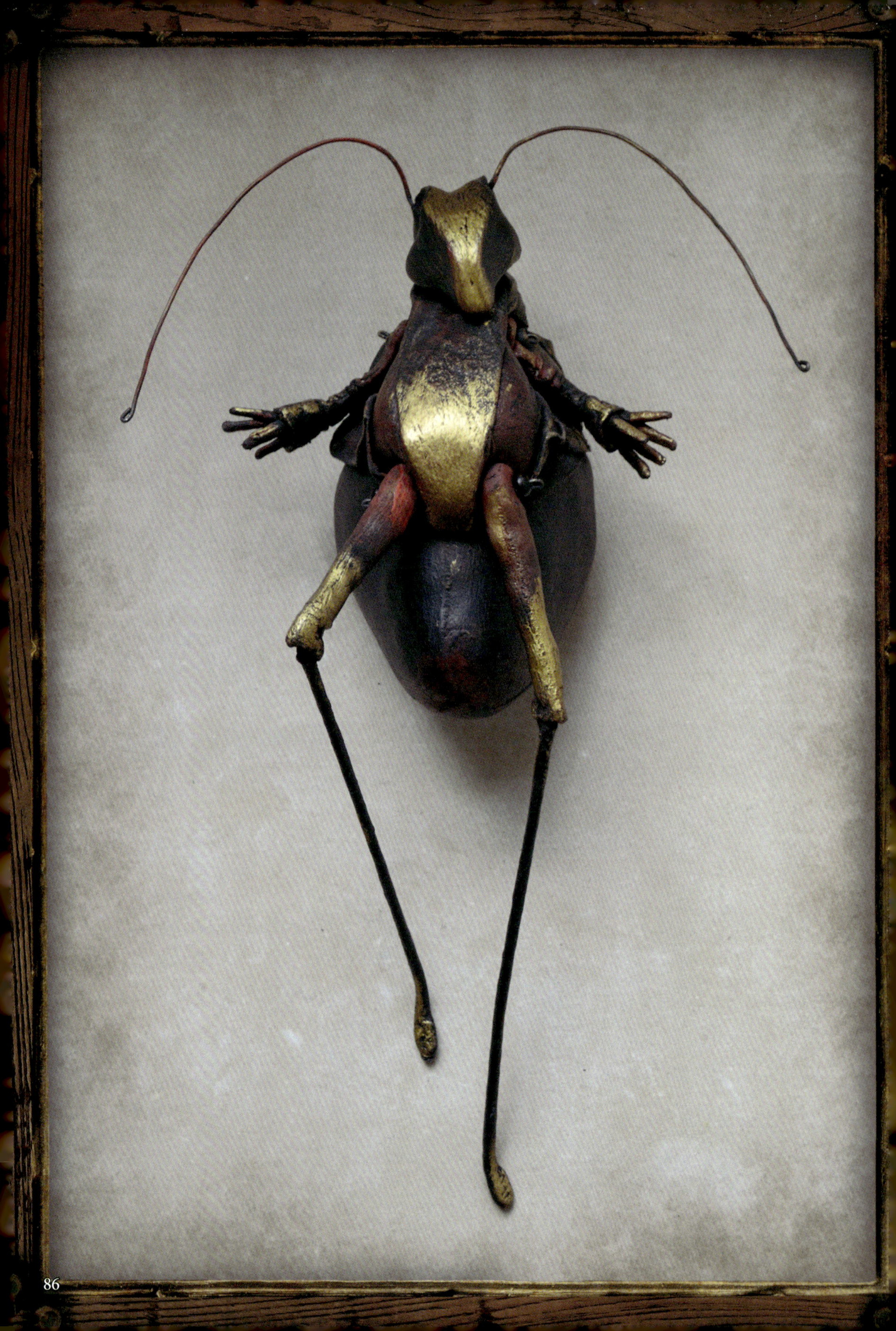

87

88

Gardenia Lantern

89

Twice

One of the most common questions we are asked at the museum is, 'Can a Figment be brought back to life if given another dose of the Potion of the Circle?'*

The simple answer is yes. But this is not something any respectable witch would ever talk about, let alone do. The act of reanimating a Figment is only ever considered when a witch has died or gone missing under strange circumstances... or if a dark witch has been using magic improperly.

Then, and only then, is the Figment revived, in the hope they can help with enquiries.

This is known as a *Twice*.

Whilst initially appearing normal, Figments who are given the Potion of the Circle a second time soon spiral out of control, with strange and erratic behaviour. They evolve into compulsive thieves of small objects; they pinch and hoard, often tying their loot to themsleves with string, which quickly becomes dirty and tangled.

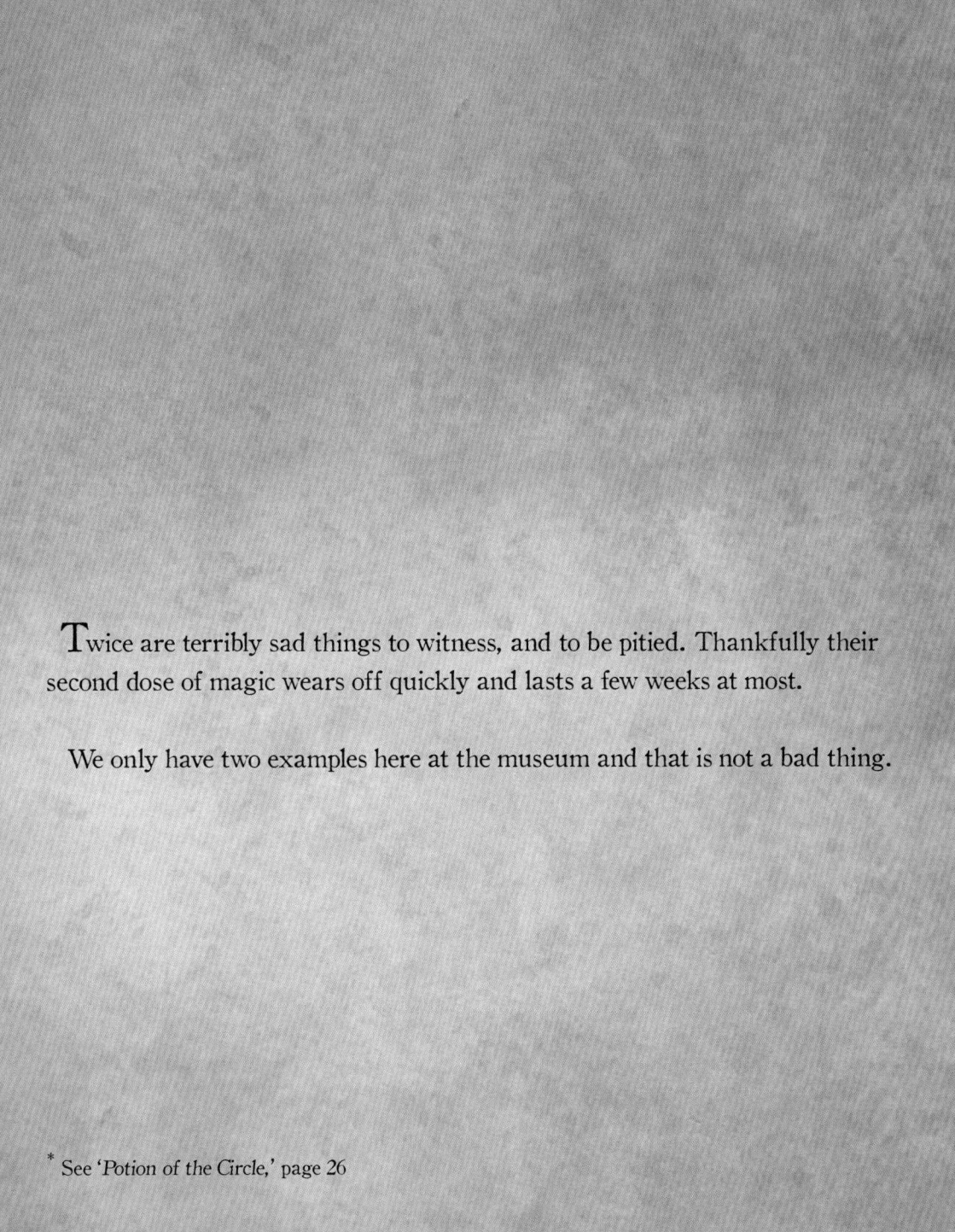

Twice are terribly sad things to witness, and to be pitied. Thankfully their second dose of magic wears off quickly and lasts a few weeks at most.

We only have two examples here at the museum and that is not a bad thing.

* See 'Potion of the Circle,' page 26

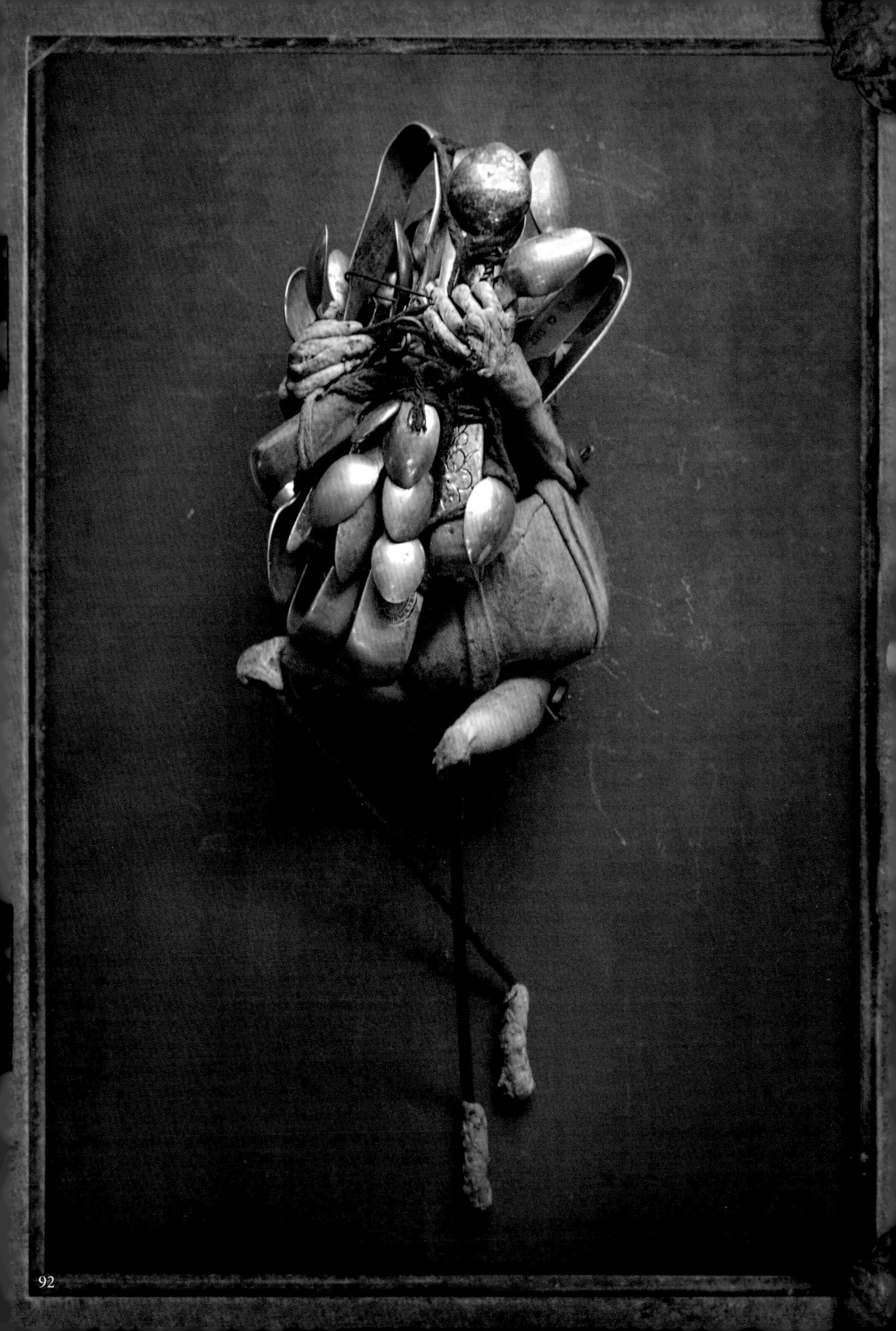

93

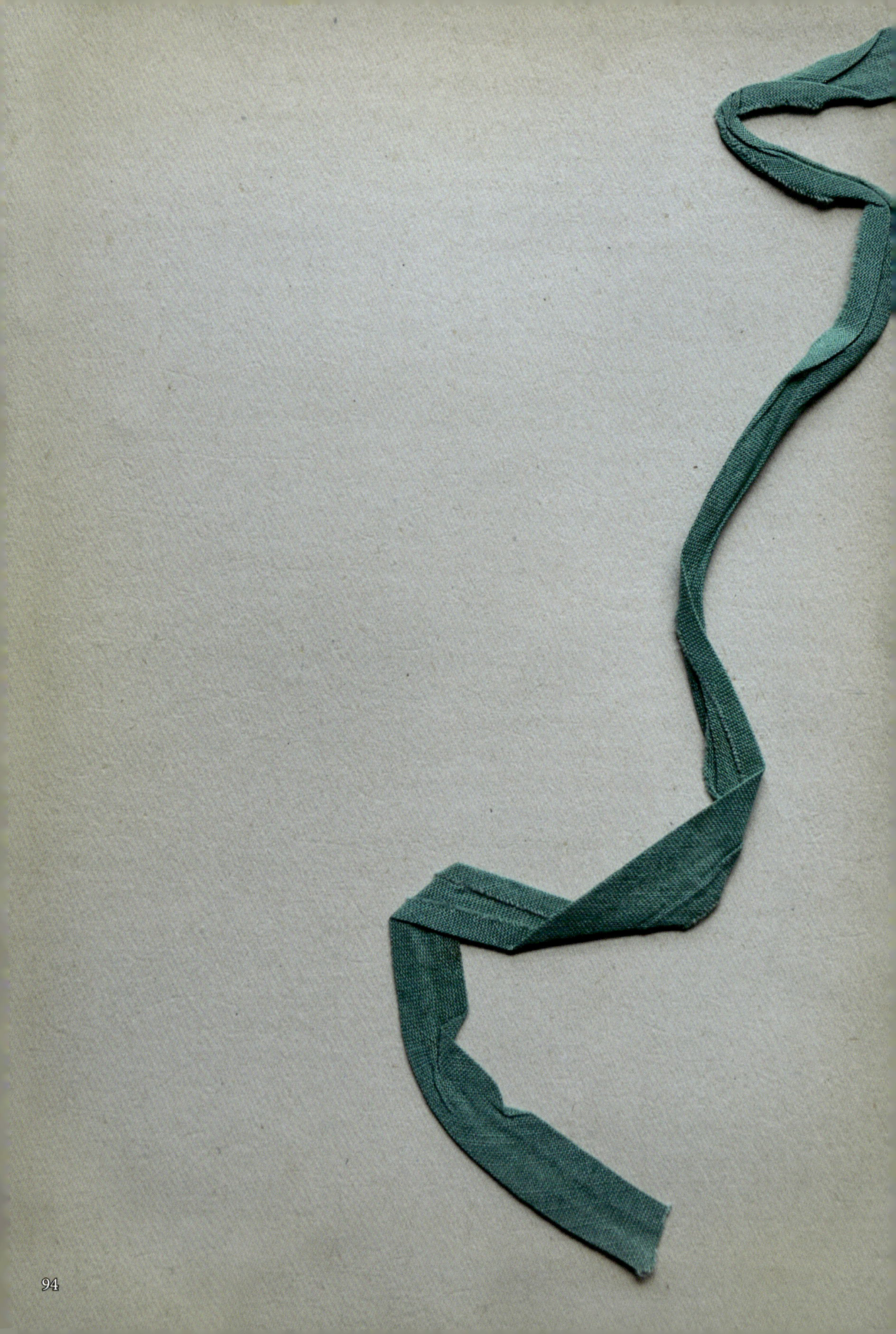

Some of the strangest and most fantastical of the Figment family, these incredibly fast runners are exceptional at their role of delivering and collecting.

Hidden compartments and drawers within their bodies enable them to hold jars and objects safely whilst travelling at lightning speed.

Cupboardys are a huge help to a witch who chooses a lonelier path or lives in a remote location.

Highly active at night they are known to travel in small groups, retrieving and transporting potions and private correspondences.

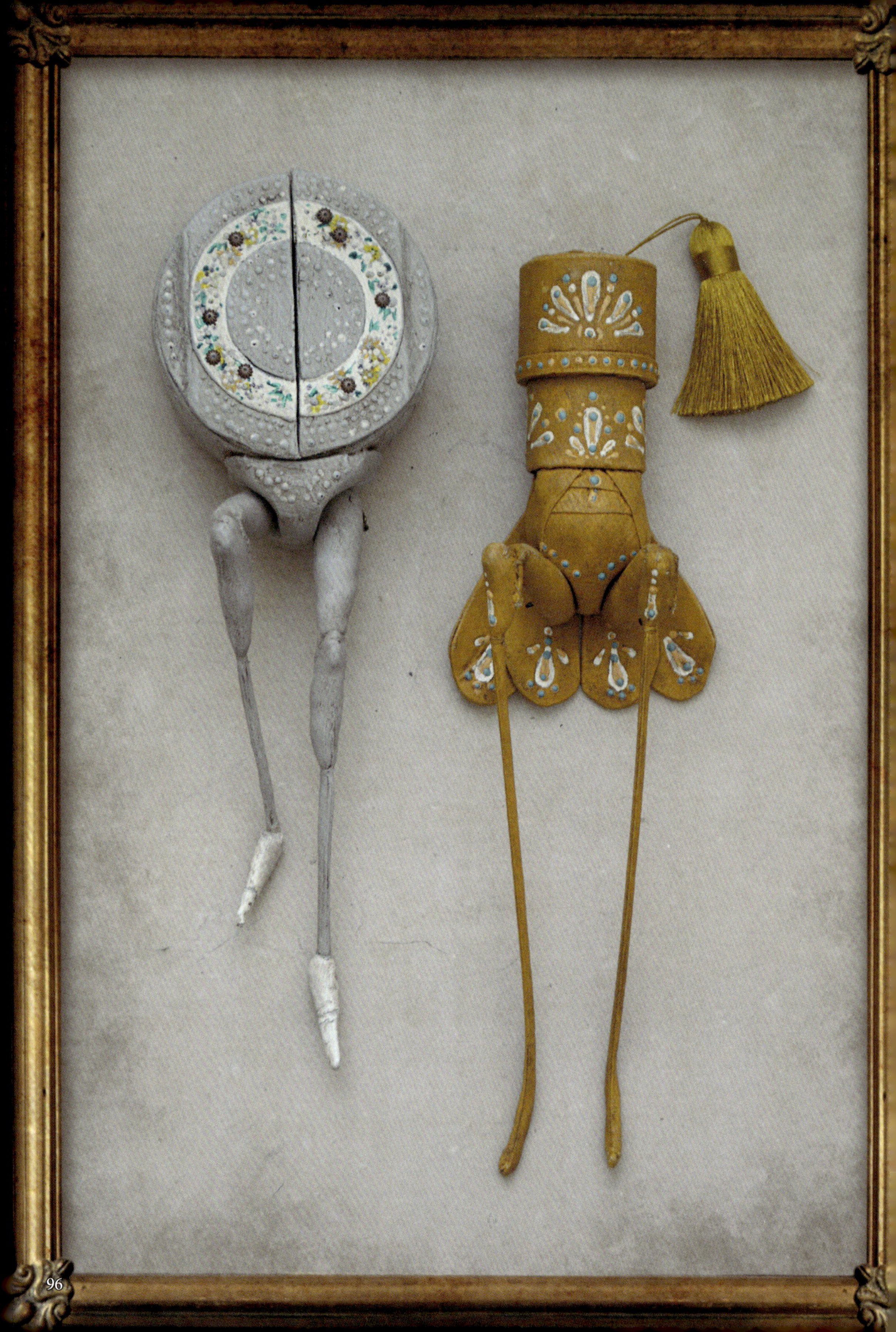

97

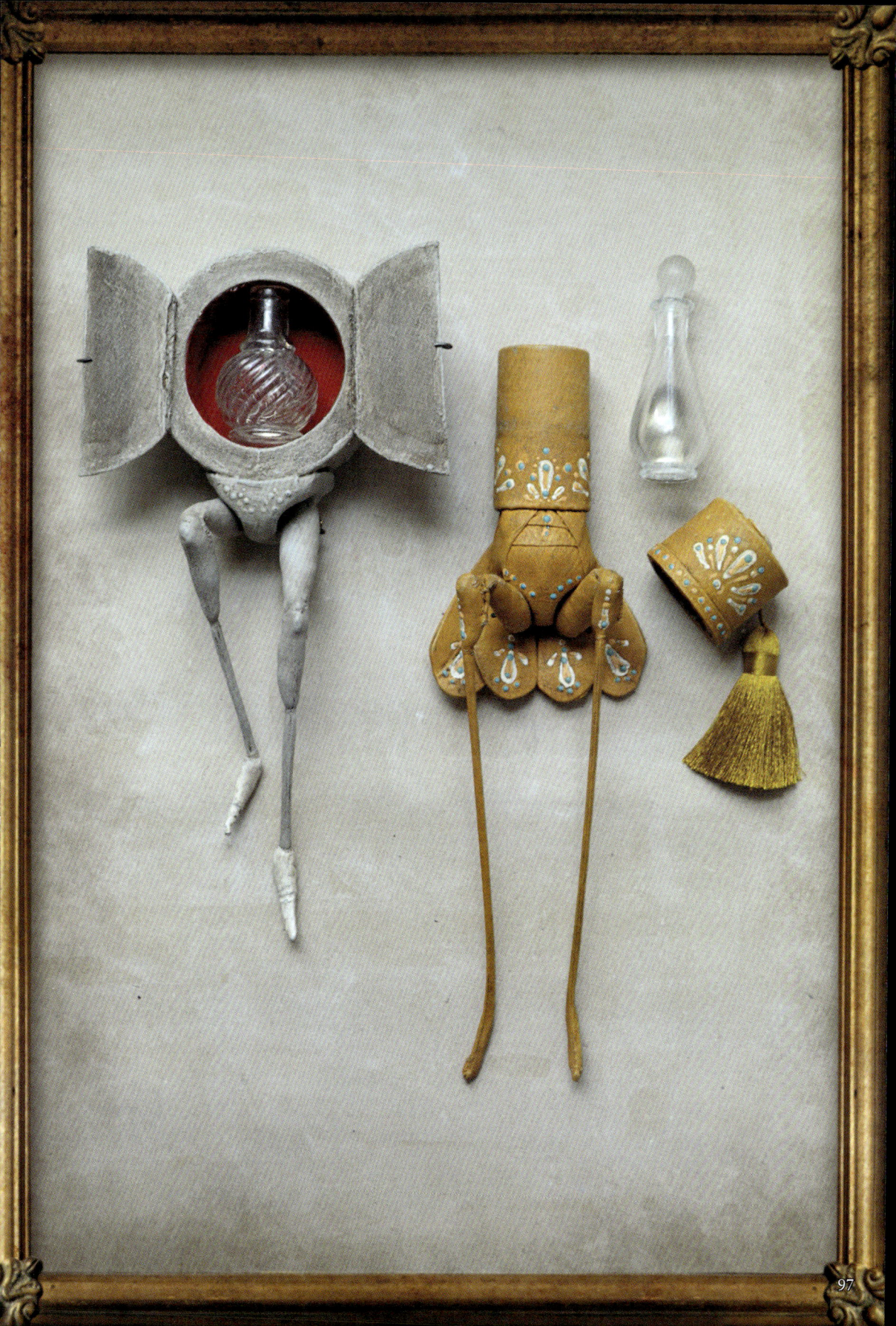

98

99

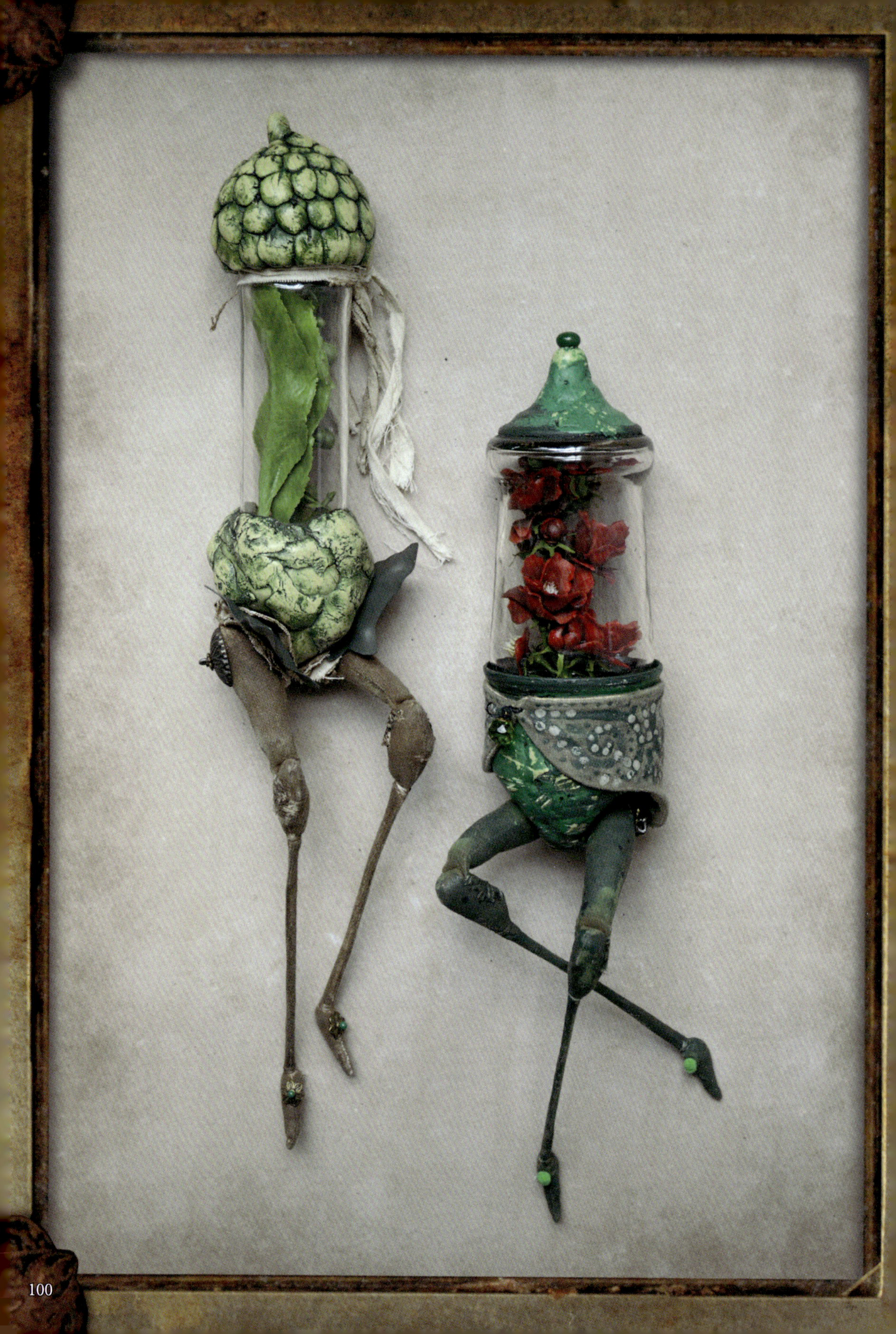

101

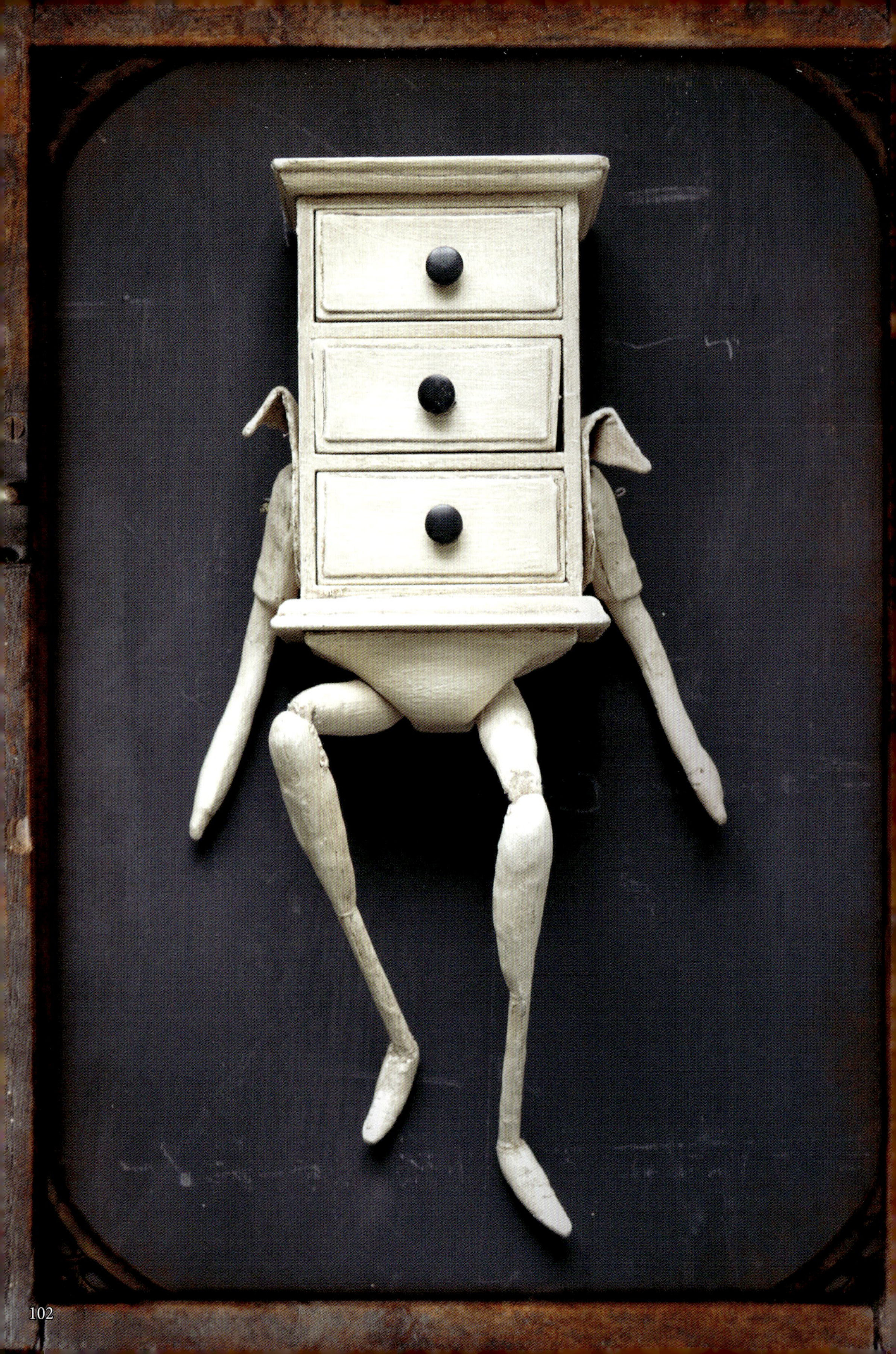

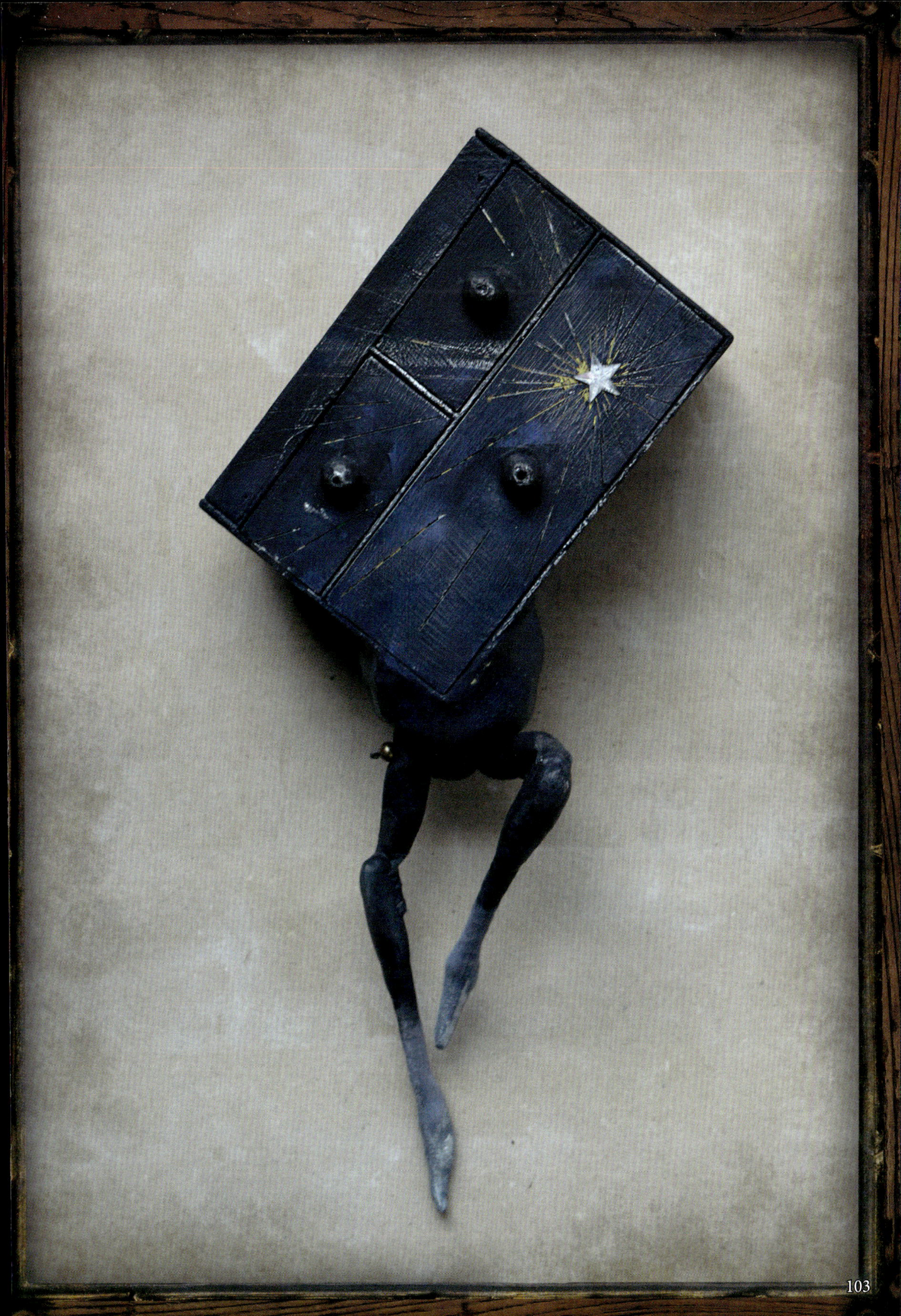

104

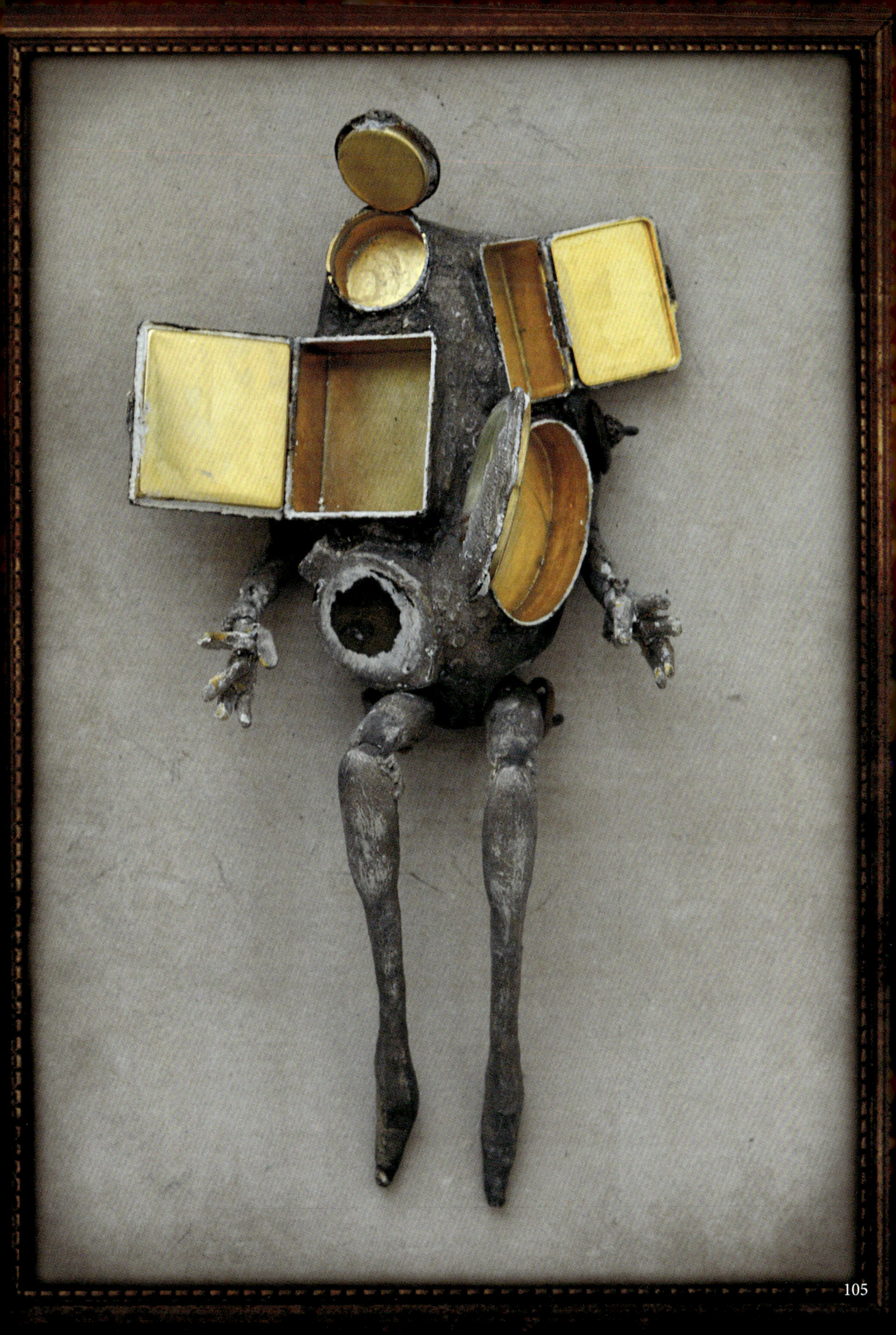

106

107

108

109

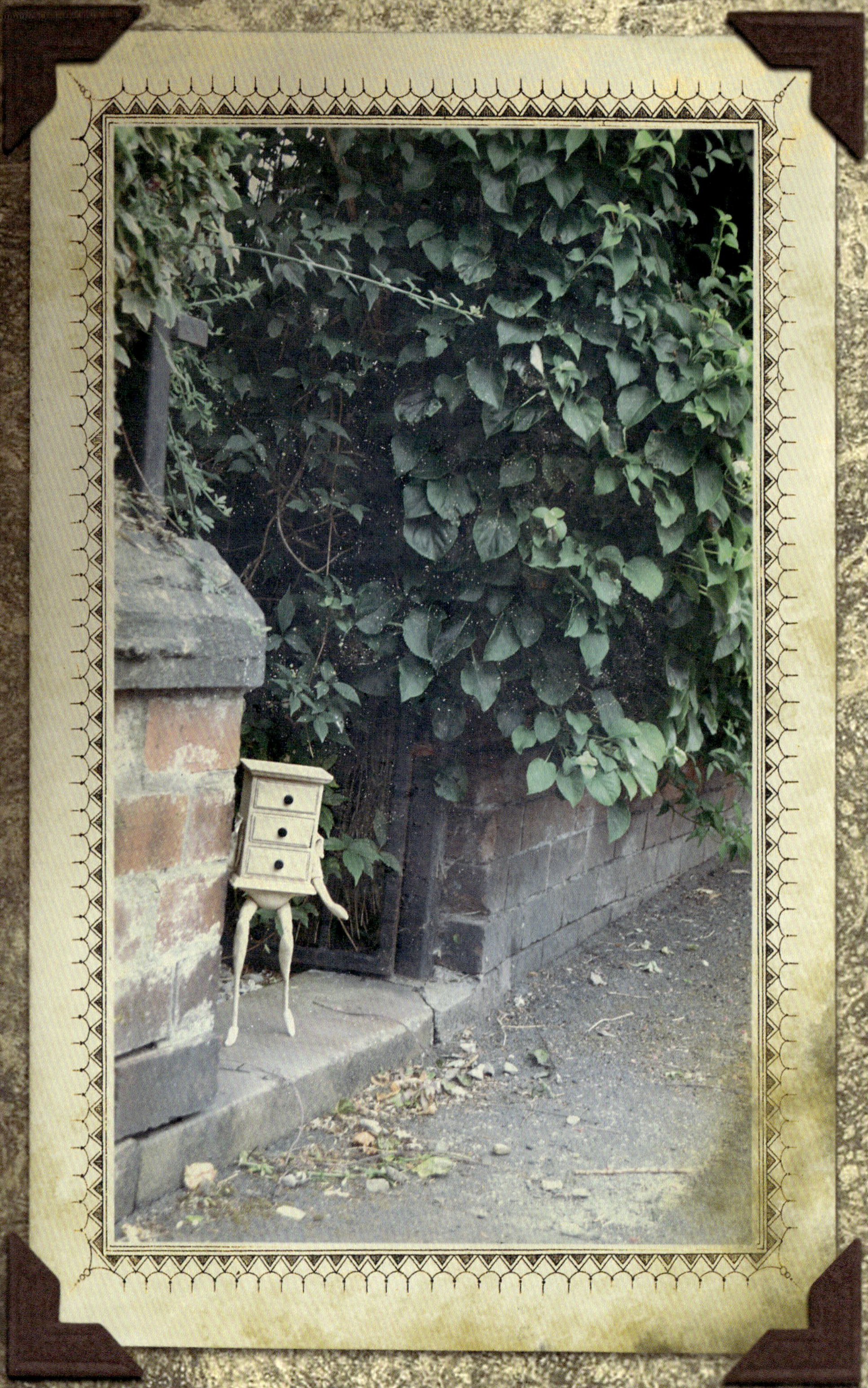

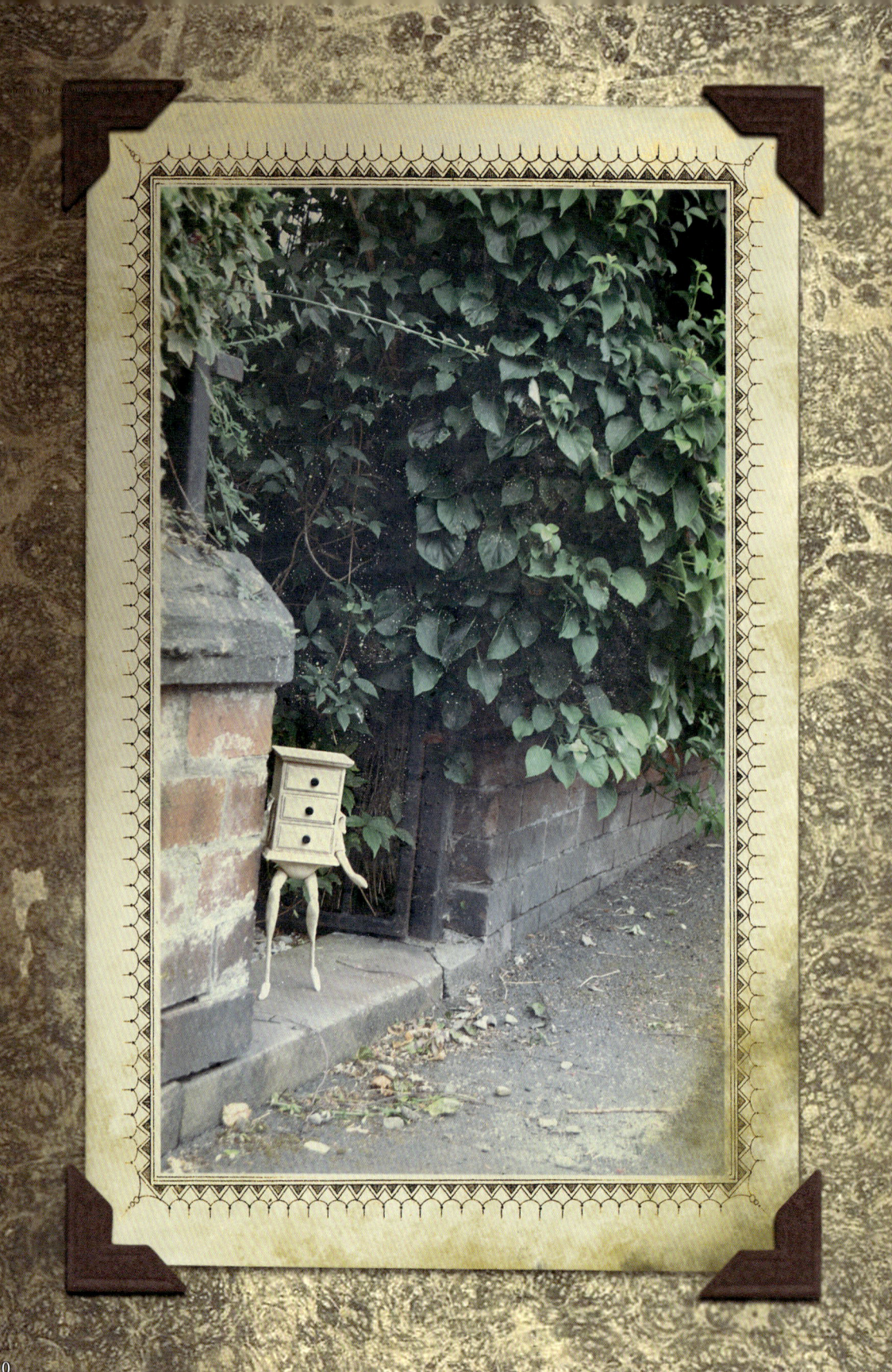

POTION BOTTLES

used by Cupboardys

111

Candle Snuffer Wands

The use of candle snuffers as wands is not unique to Thimble Witches but it does seem to be more common within this family of magic workers.

Particularly useful in drawing out magic patterns in the earth and sand, they are held backwards with the snuffer in the palm and the stem pointing out.

Most are made from metal, usually brass, and are often elaborate in design. Very early examples are made from twigs and shells.

Snuffers are traditionally given to a young witch who is leaving home or embarking upon a long journey.

The tapping of the end to create a ringing sound is said to draw the attention of fairy folk who will help guide a witch who is lost or needs help locating ingredients.

Cone snuffers without a stem are often used to measure out spell ingredients.

Interestingly, when Thimble Witches marry the cake is often topped with a snuffer made with icing. It is said to represent both the Thimble – hard working individuals; and the Snuffer – a long, measured journey through life, together.

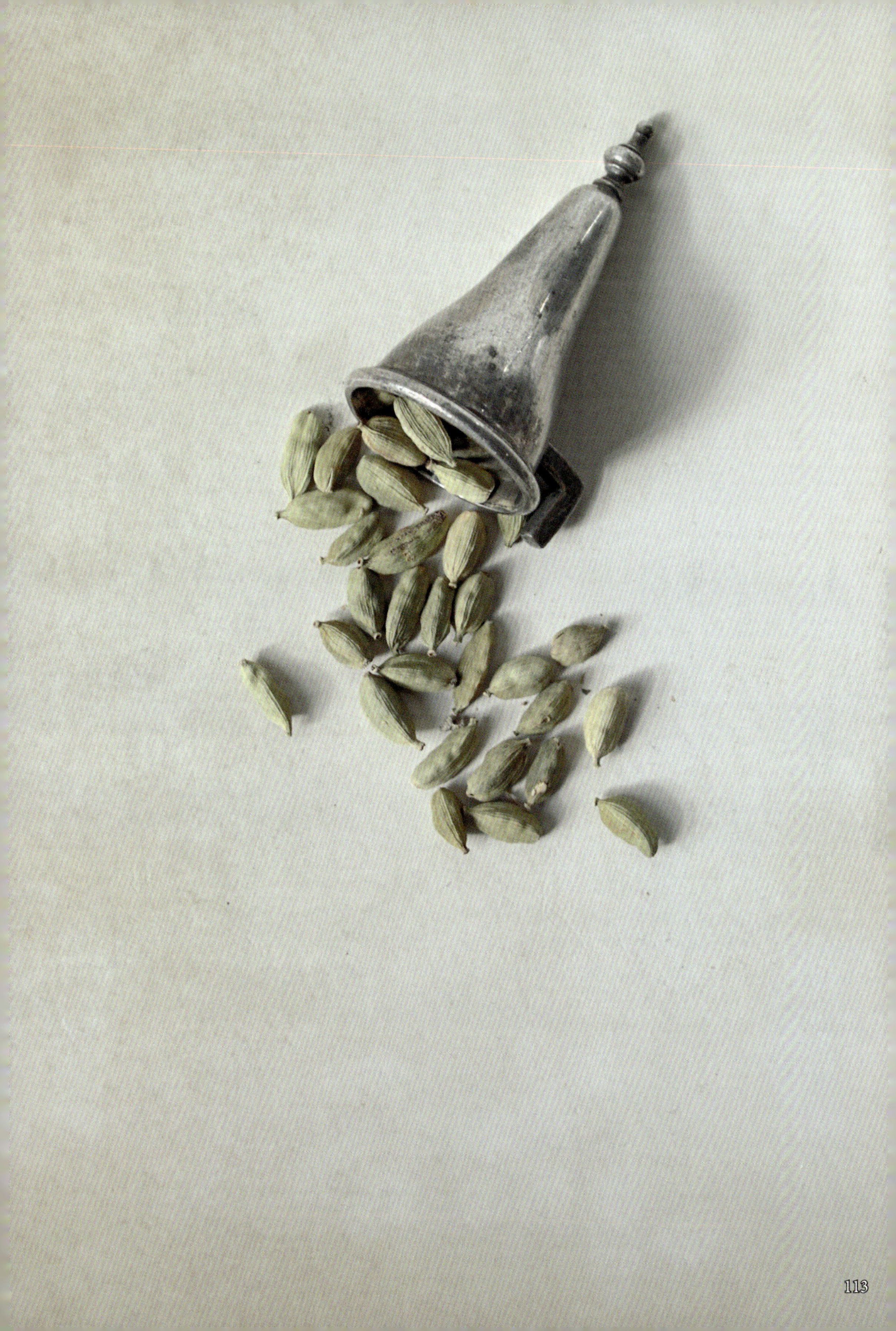

114

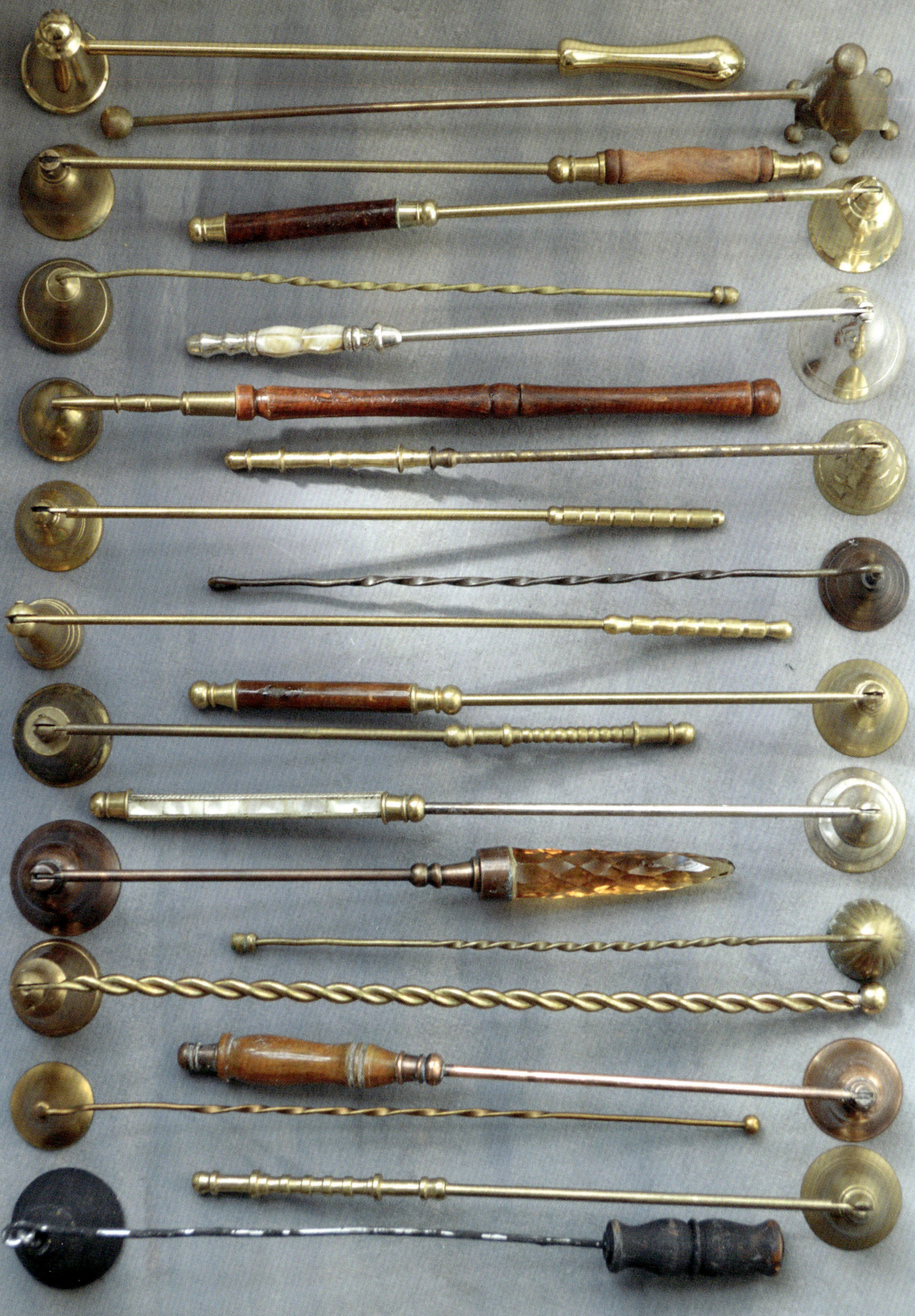

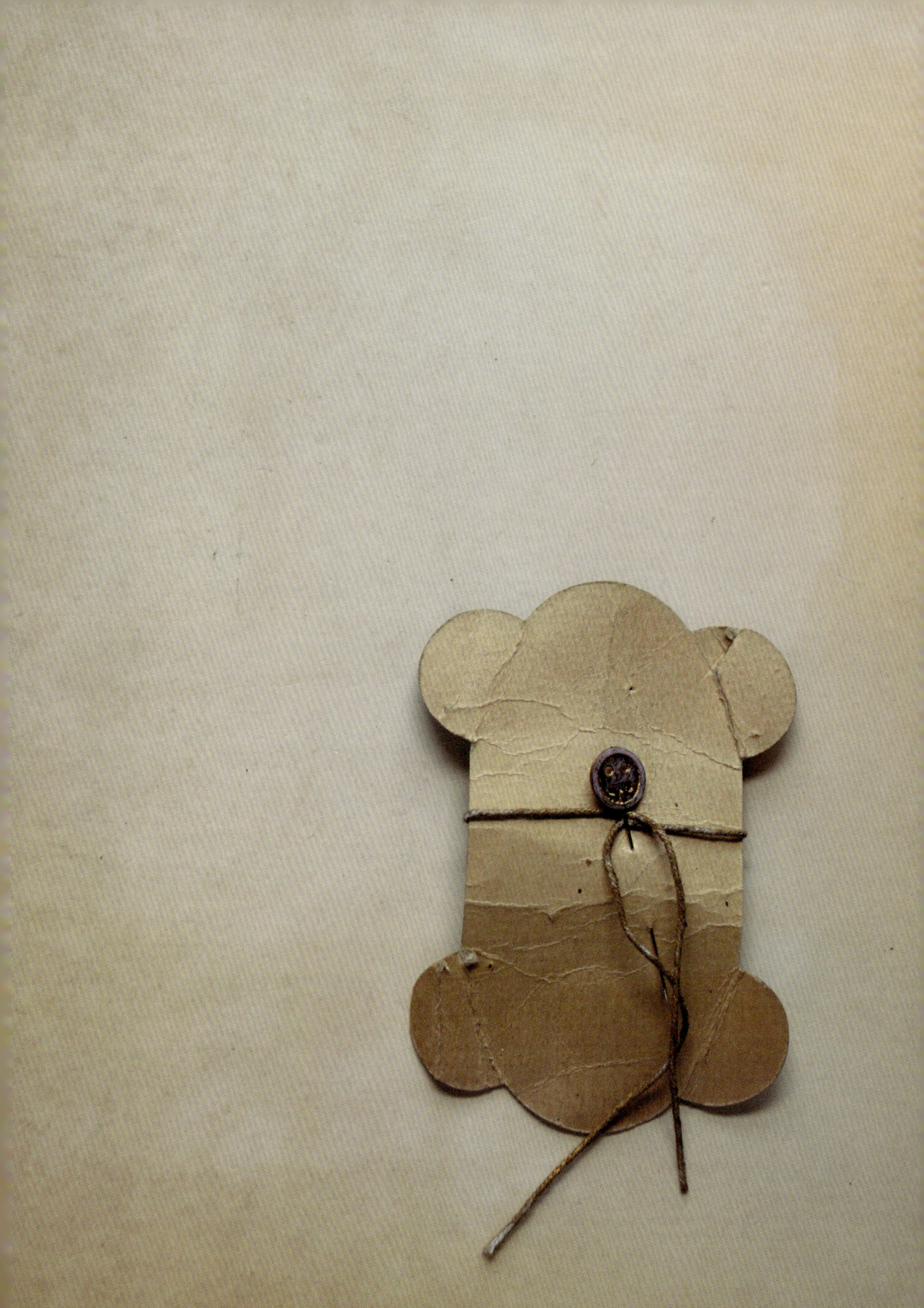

Stories

Some Figments just don't seem to fit into any particular category and that's what makes them some of our favourites.

We believe that some are companions, offering friendship to the loneliest witches. Some are storytellers, tucking a witch up in bed at night while weaving a wonderful tale. And some, well they are just a mystery, one we don't try to understand. It doesn't make them any less charming.

Stories are exceptional, they always light up a room with their warmth.

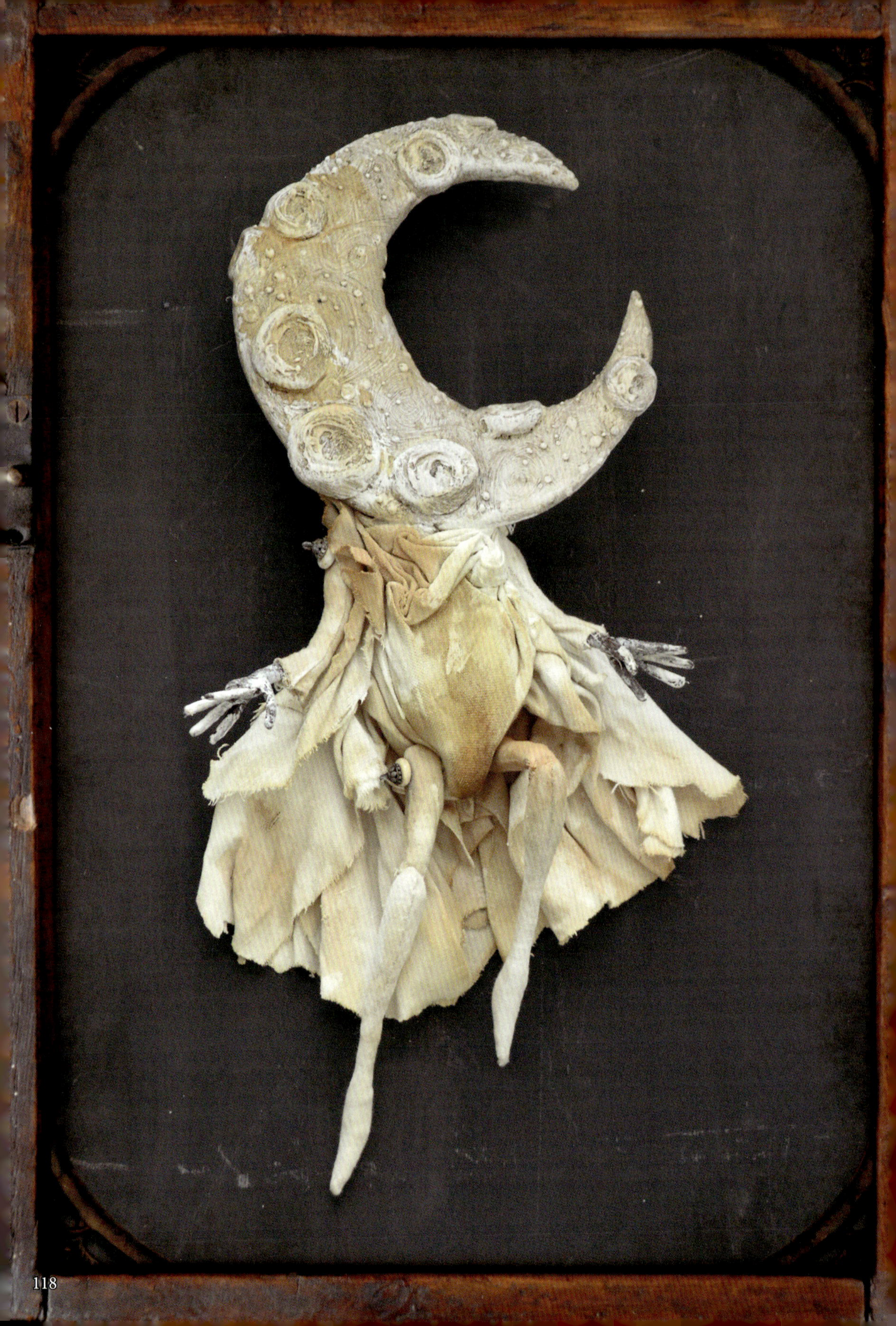

119

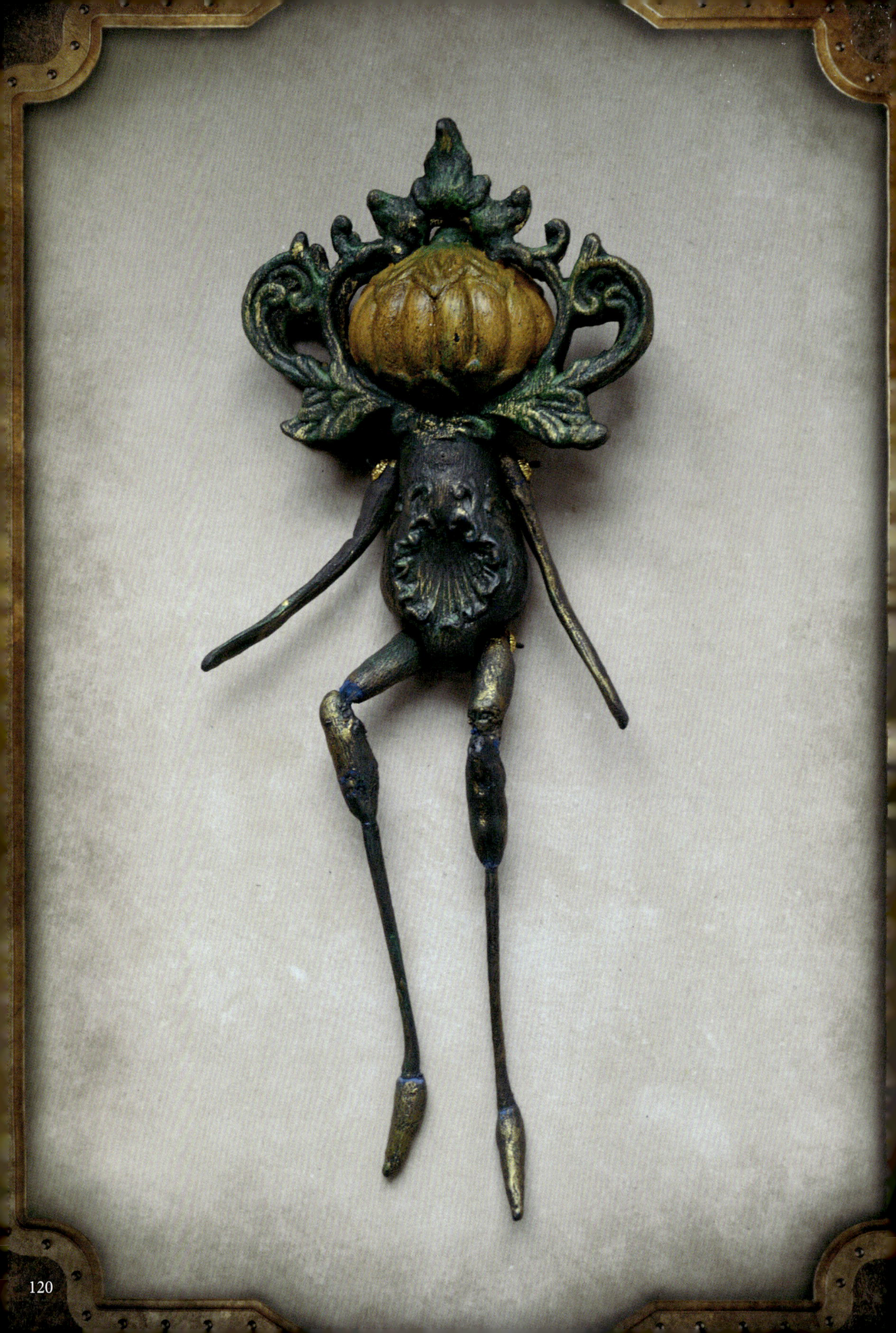

121

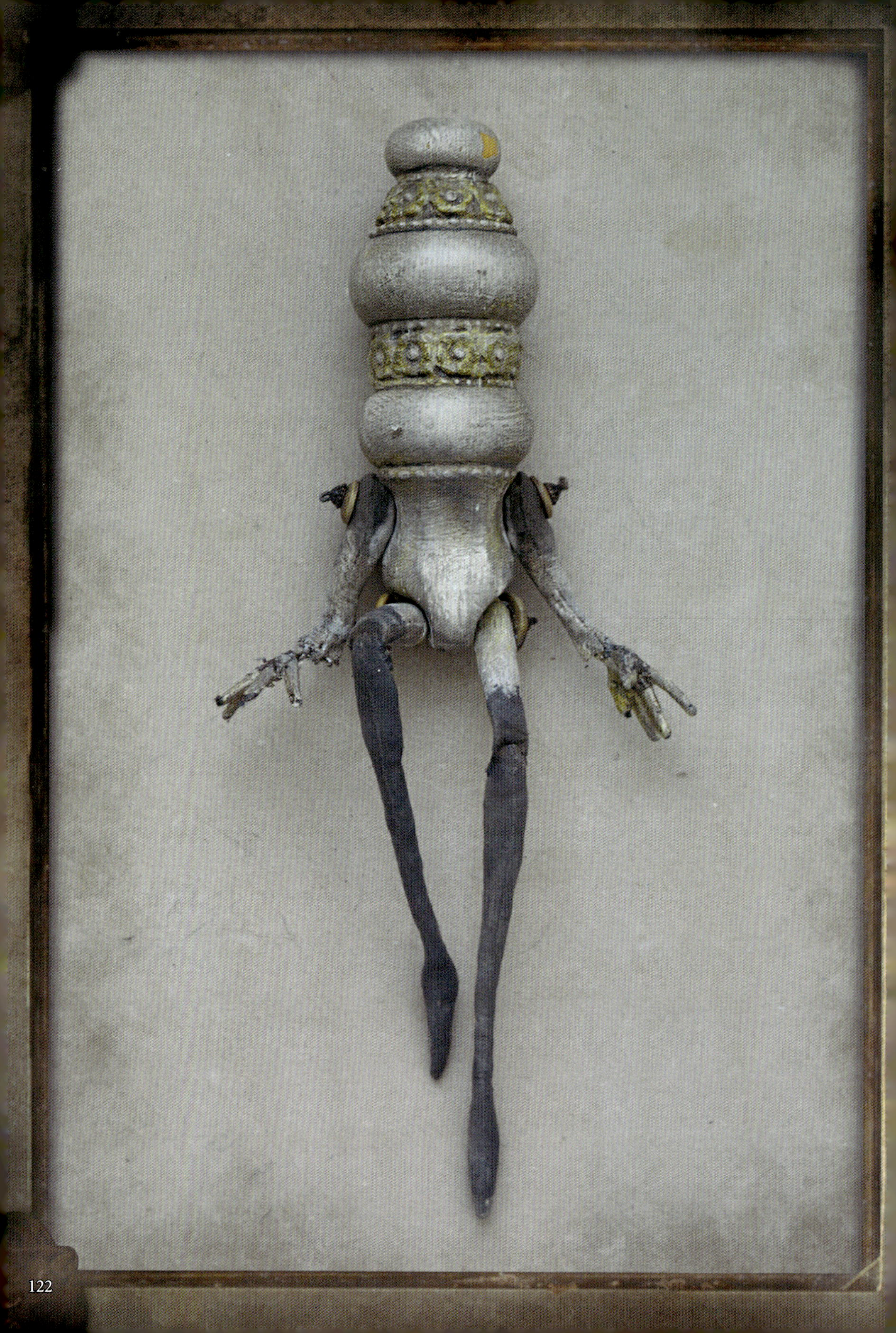

123

124

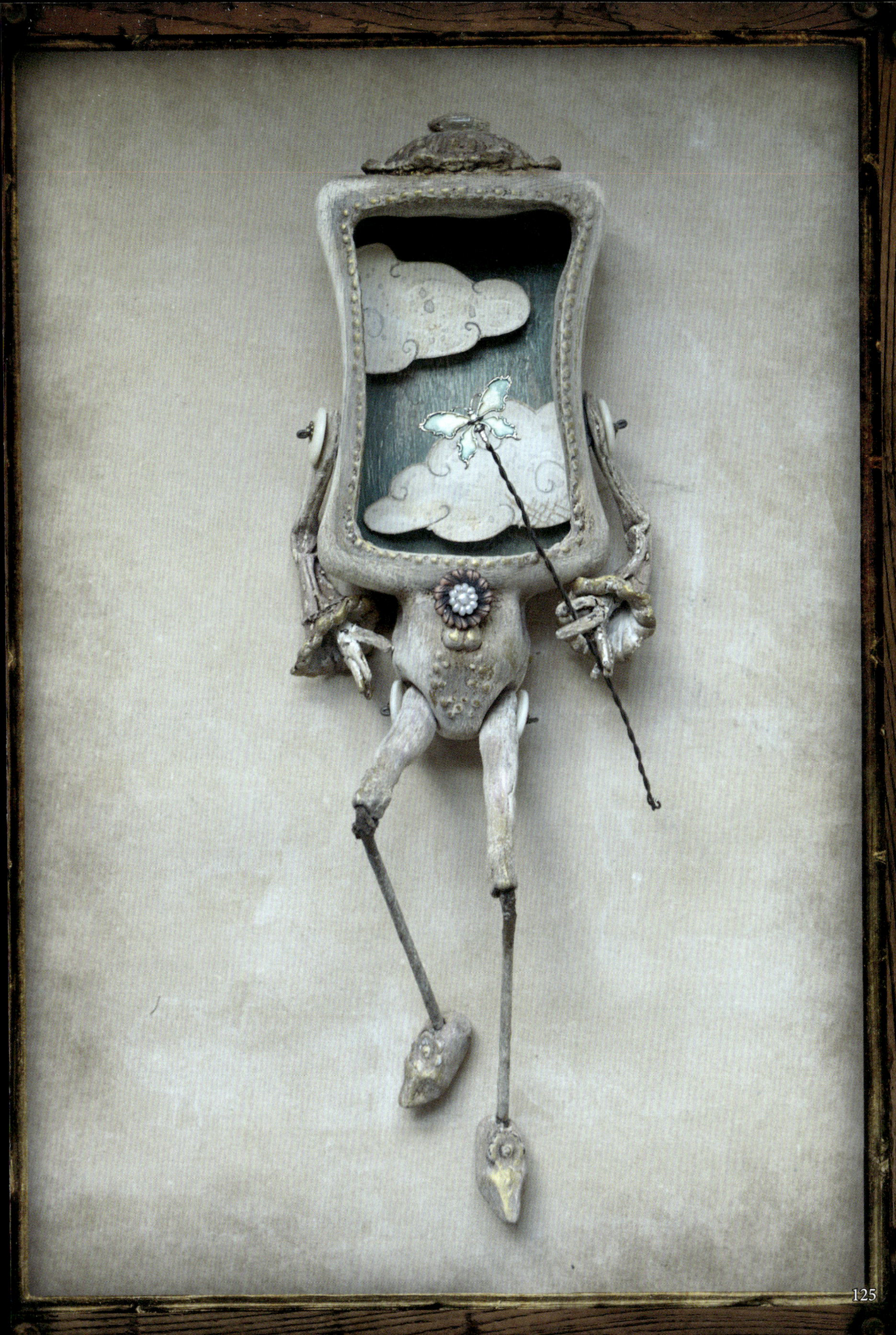

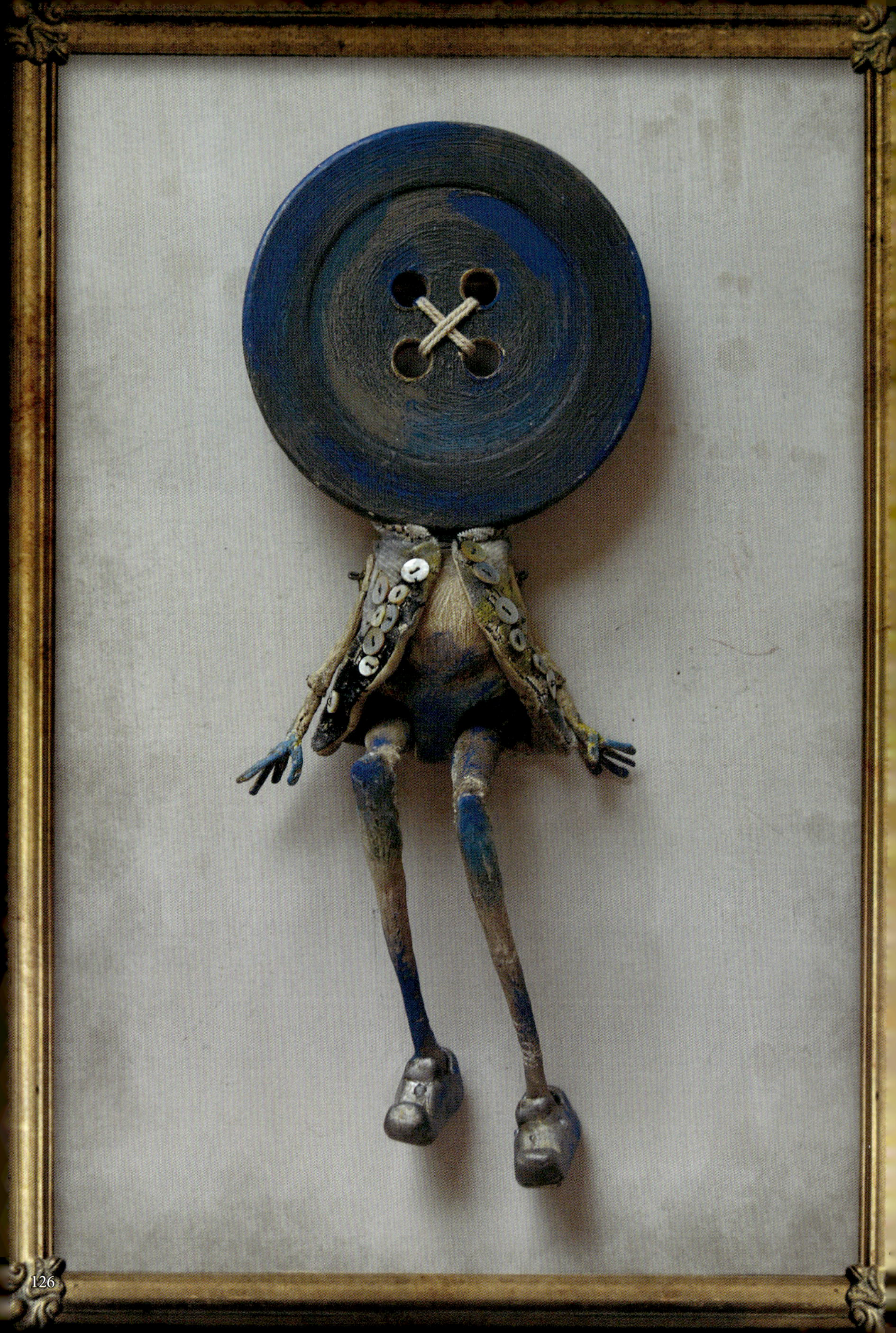

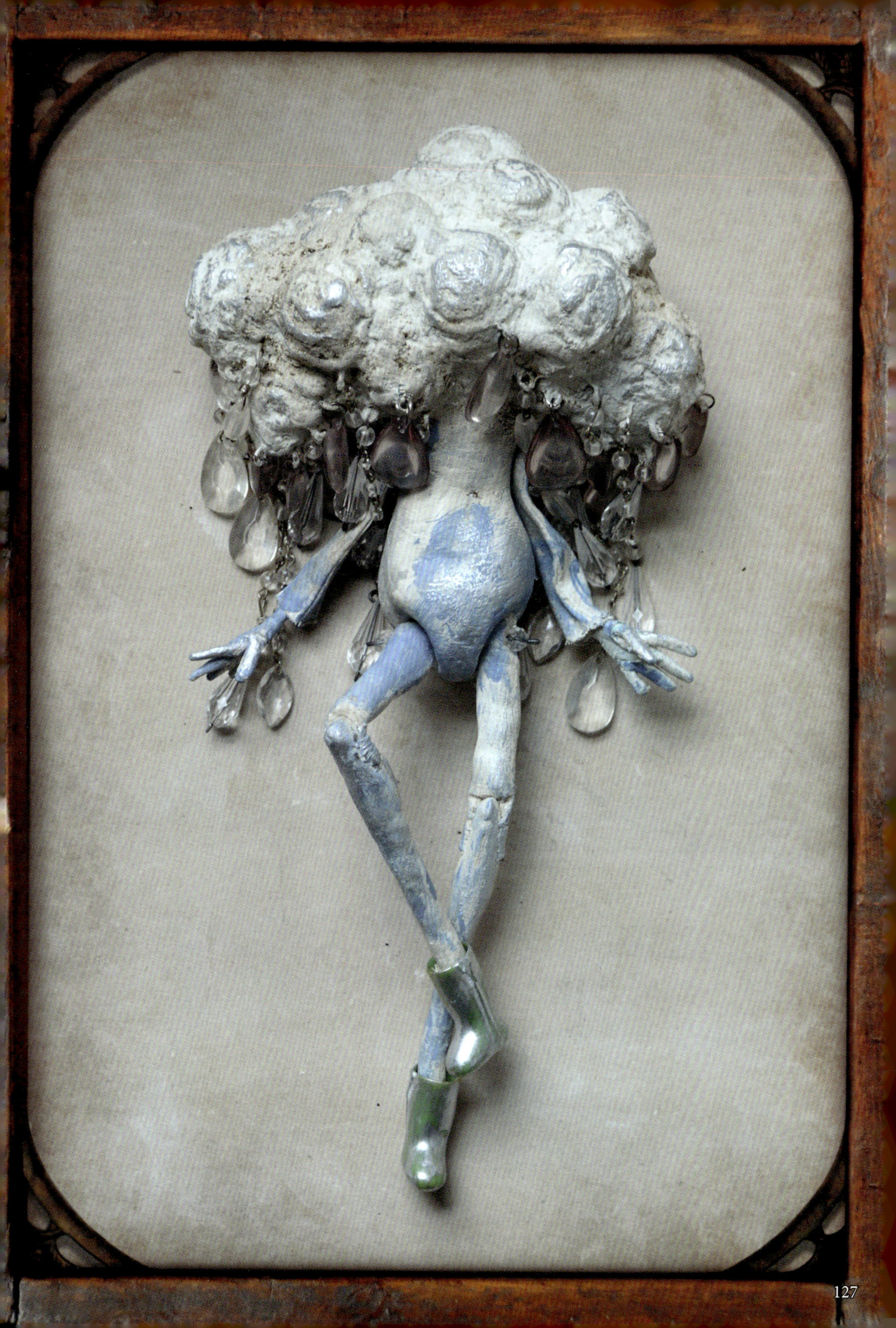

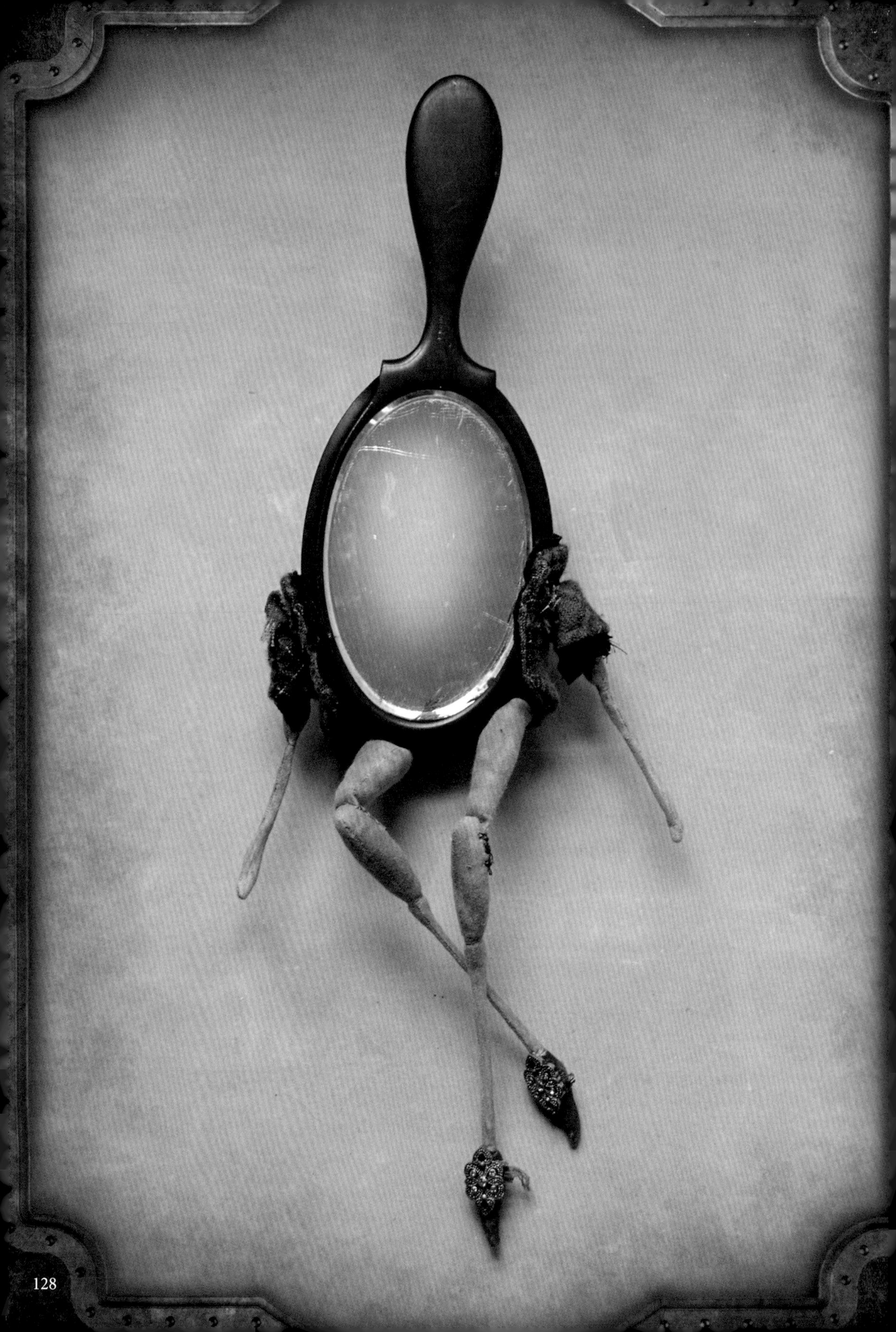

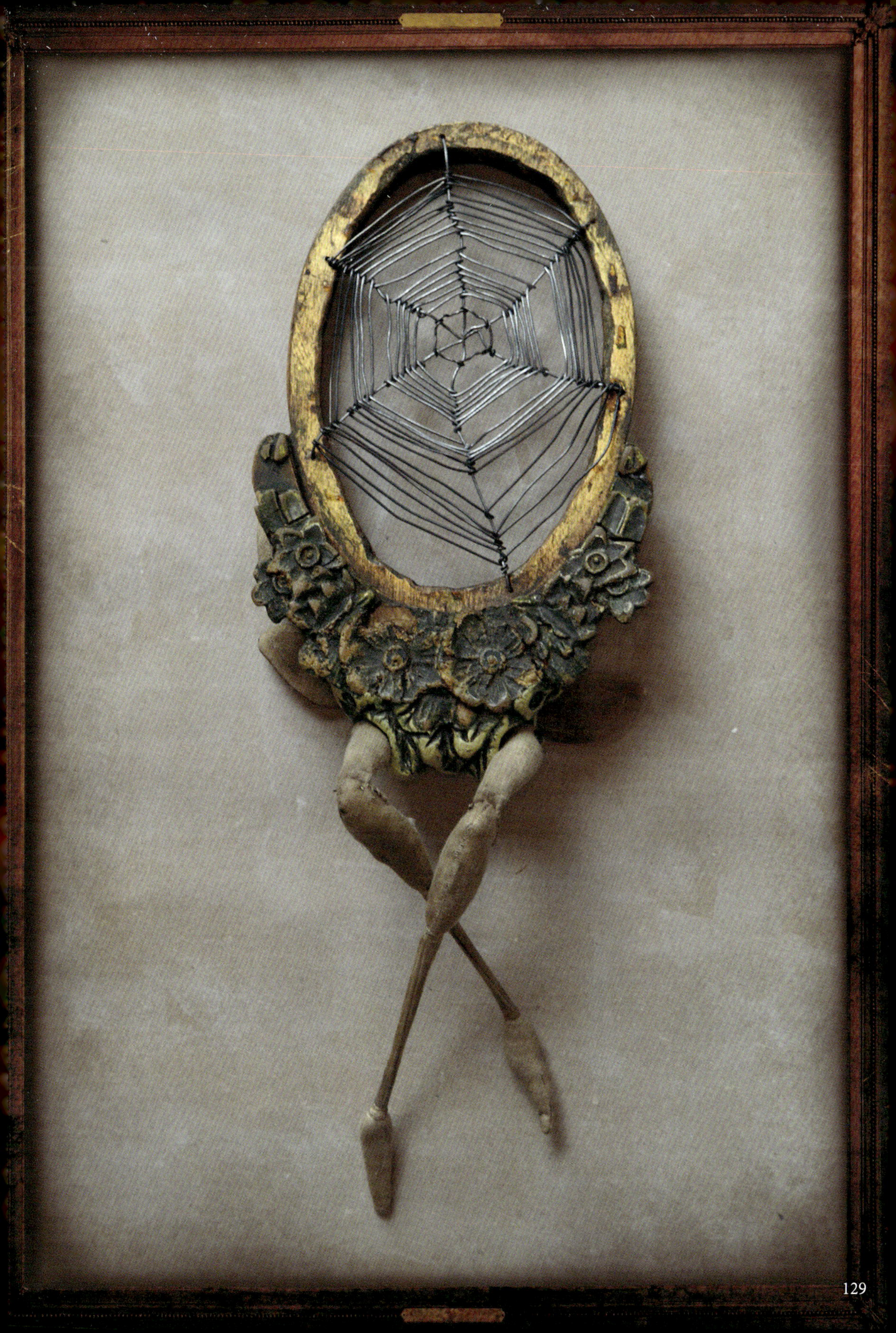

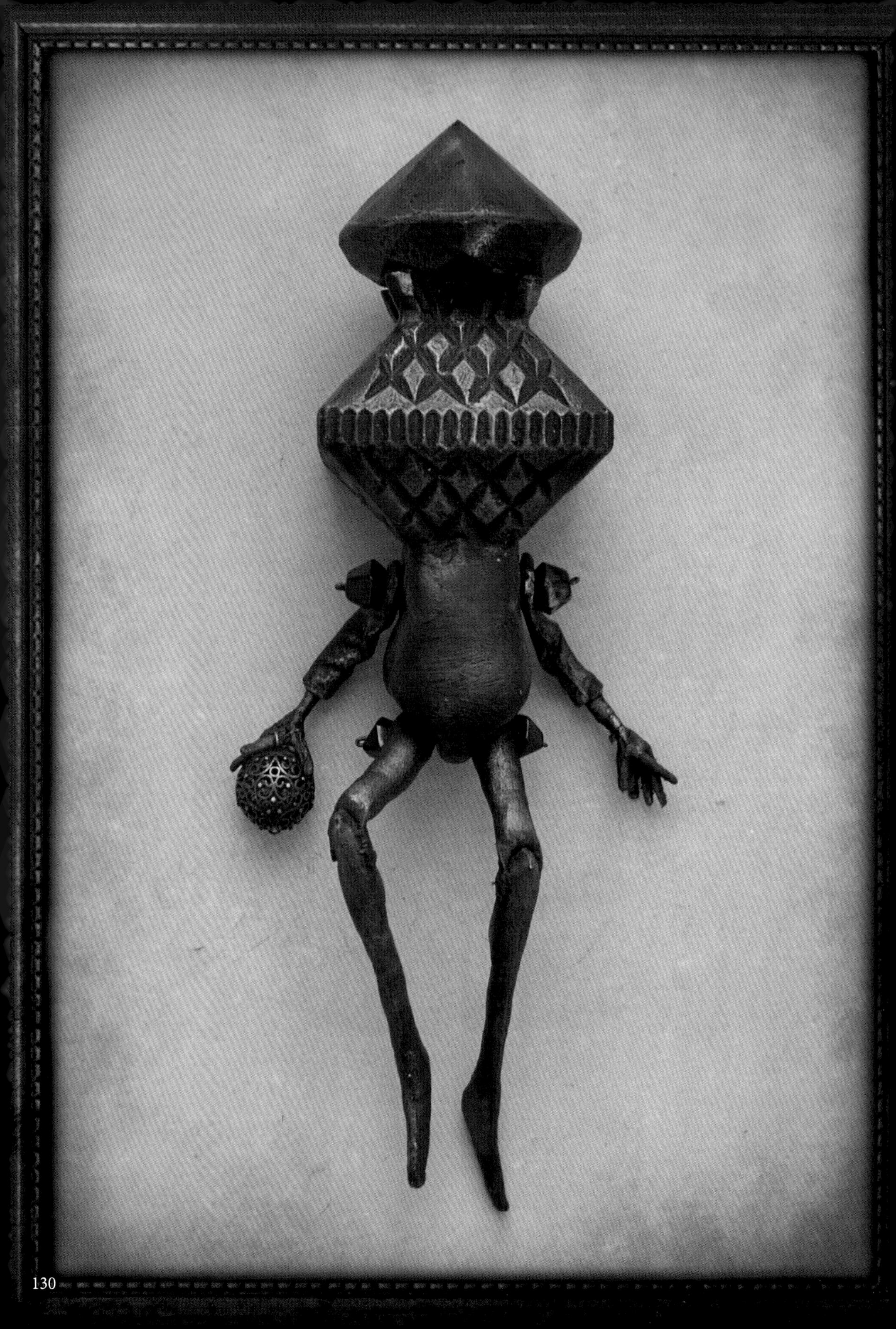

131

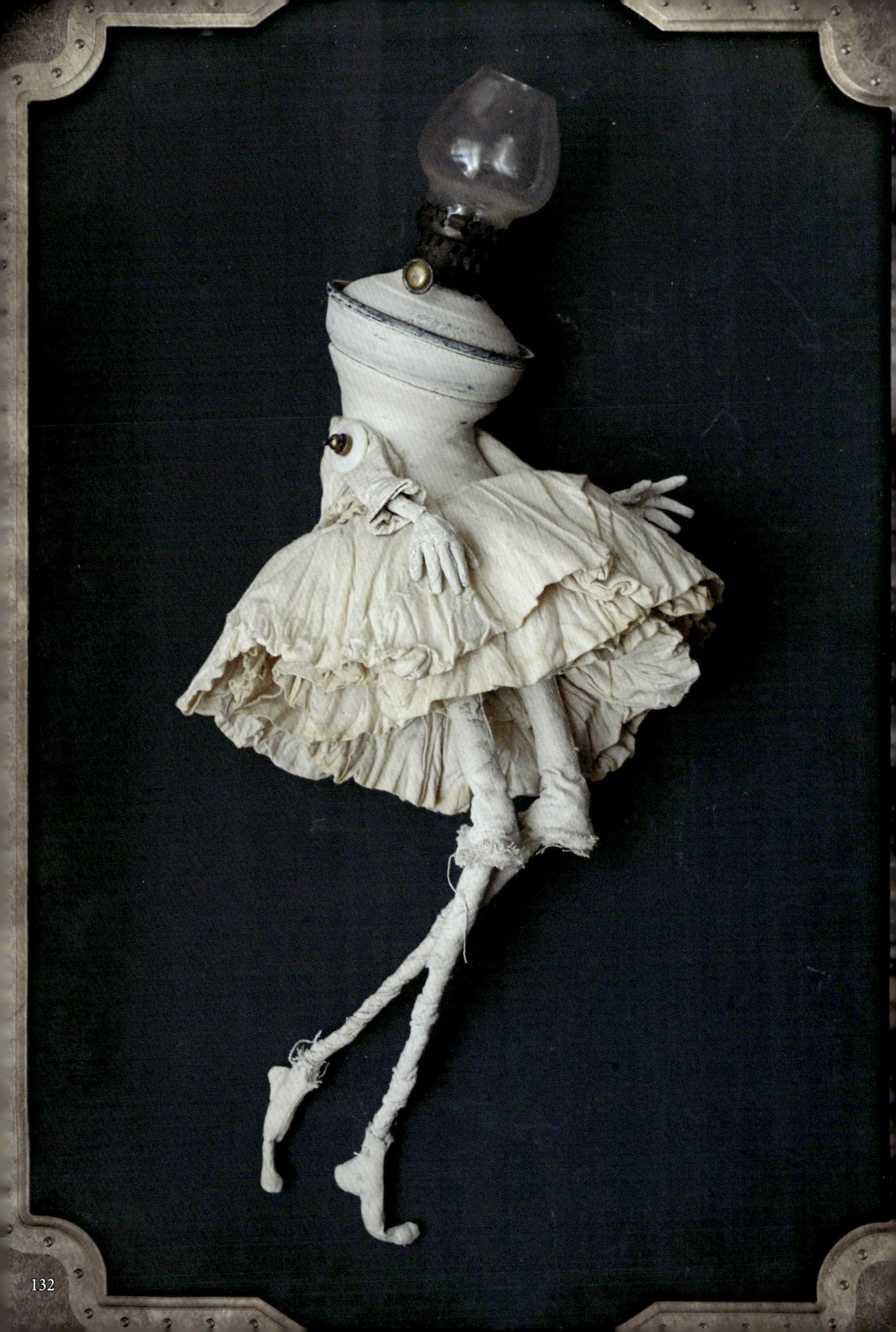

133

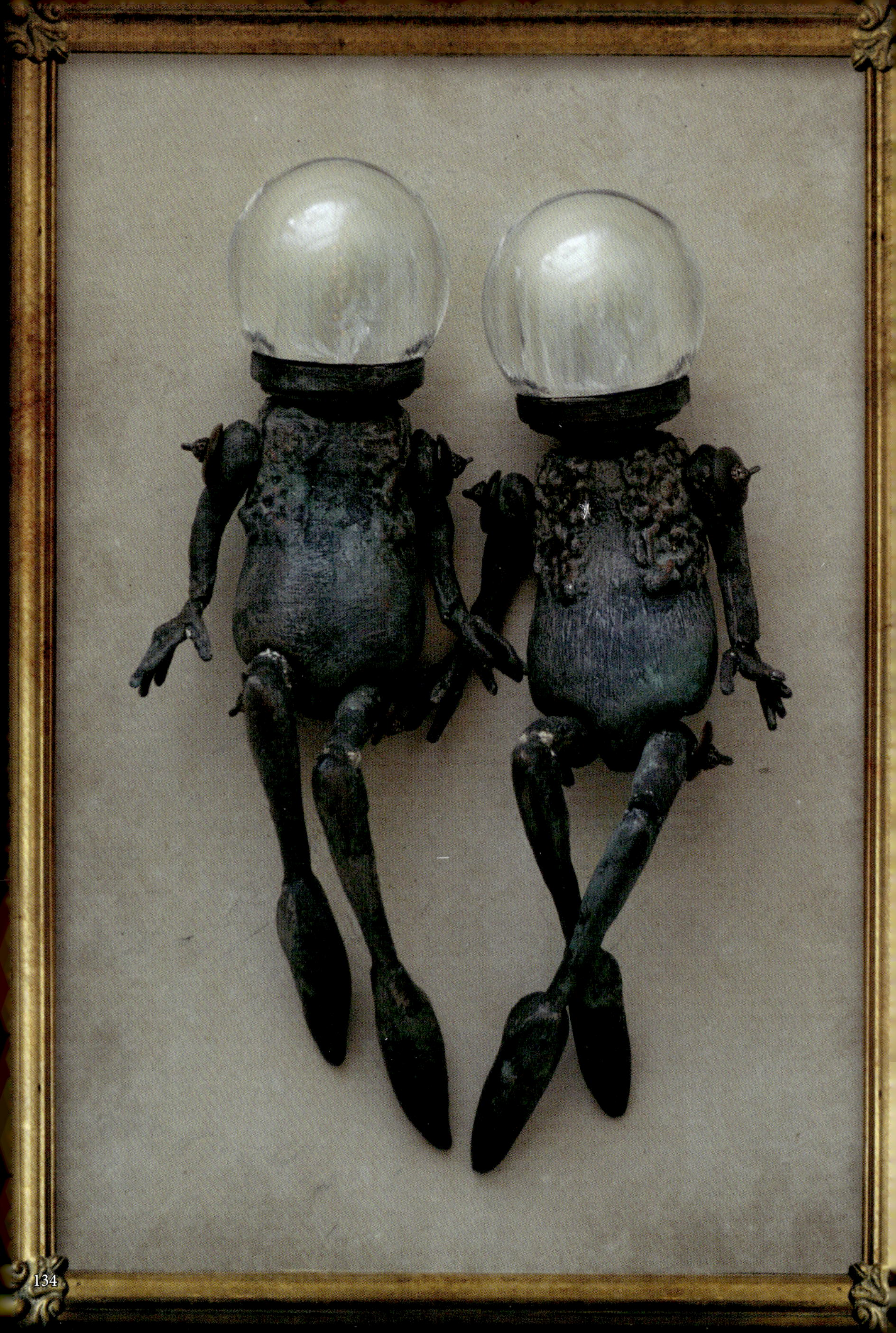

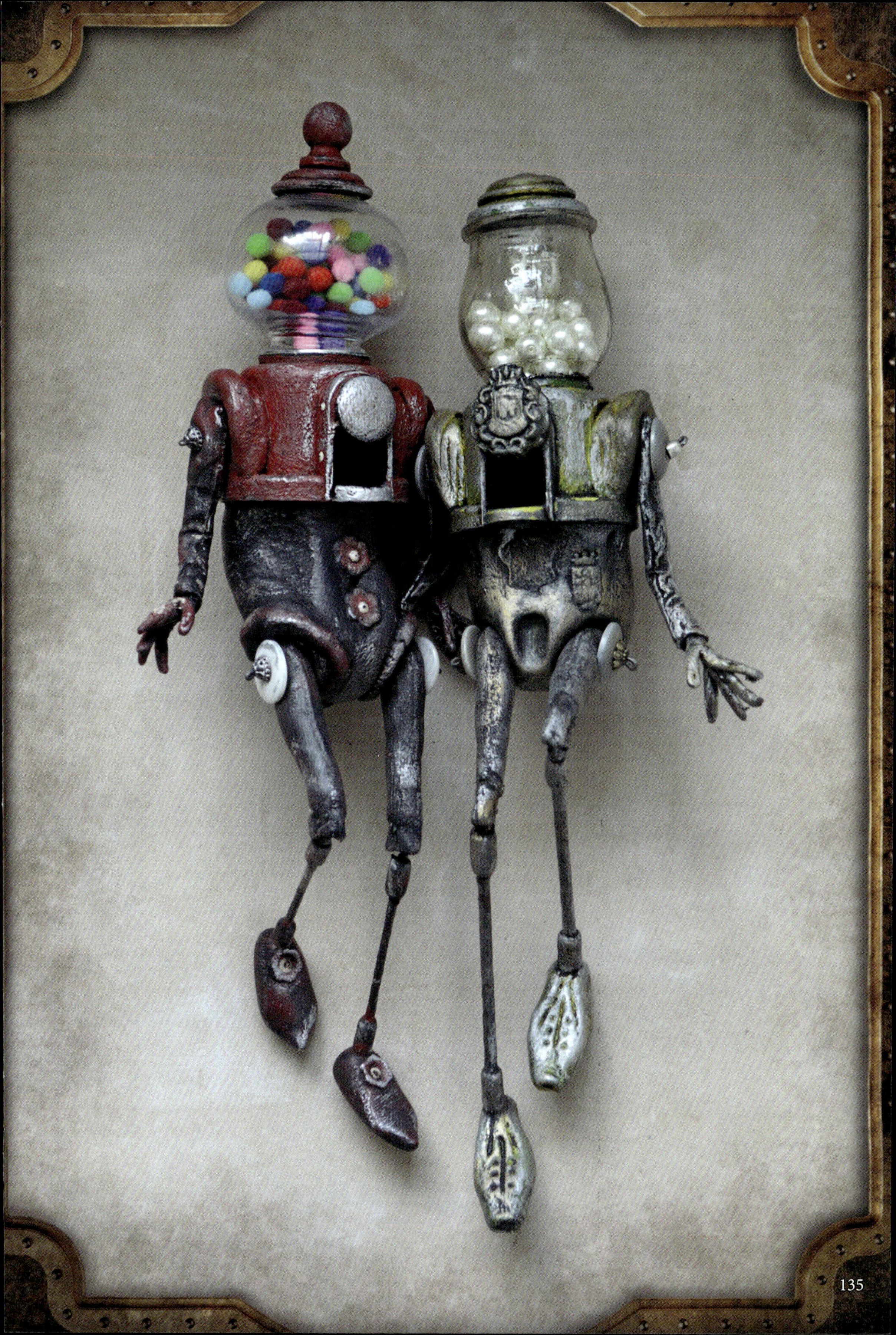

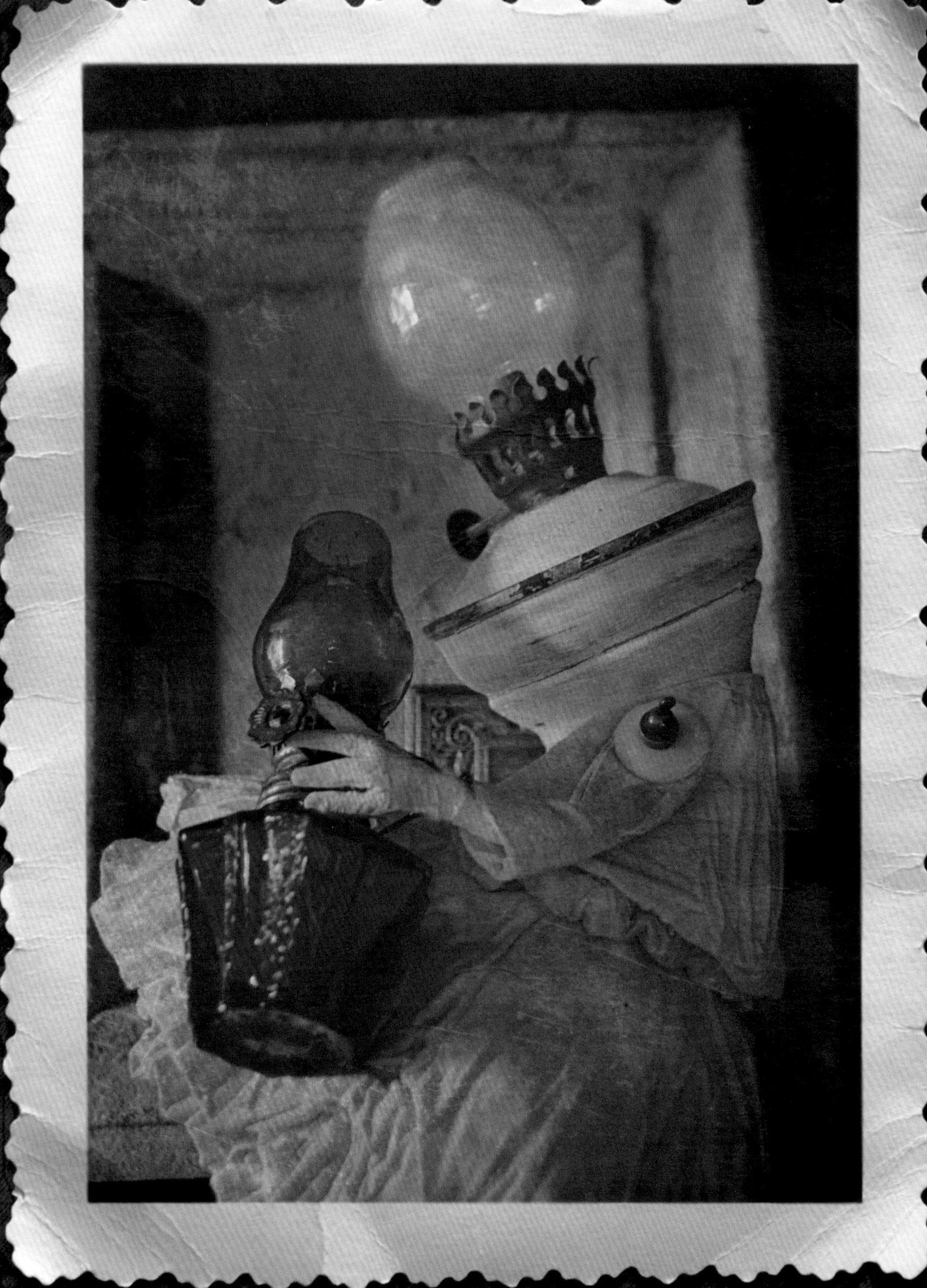

STORY BOAT
(note sails made of giant insect wings)

If you know where to look…
There is a hidden key
On a secret hook.

Go up the stairs…
and take a right…
There's a corridor lit
by candle light.

A door of red
waits for you there
use the key,
you're halfway there.

Go through the door
show your brass book
red stone ring…
and take a look…

For the place of wonder
where Figments hide
'Tis a secret place
so don't confide.

We make our helpers
The witches said
And here they rest
when we are dead.

We hope you enjoyed

The Museum of Figments

Please come again!

*Layla, Luca & Lottie...
      lots of love, Uncle Finch x*